Mom—

Thought you could use this as a refurnce for the up coming years and perhaps years past as well.

From always
your devoted son

9-9-03   Aaron

Beating the SENIOR Blues

How to Feel Better and Enjoy Life Again

Leslie Eckford, R.N., L.C.S.W. & Amanda Lambert, M.S.

Distributed in the U.S.A. by Publishers Group West; in Canada by Raincoast Books; in Great Britain by Airlift Book Company, Ltd.; in South Africa by Real Books, Ltd.; in Australia by Boobook; and in New Zealand by Tandem Press.

Copyright © 2002 by Leslie Eckford and Amanda Lambert
New Harbinger Publications, Inc.
5674 Shattuck Avenue
Oakland, CA 94609

Cover design © by Lightbourne Images
Edited by Heather Garnos Mitchener
Book design by Michele Waters

ISBN 1-57224-272-8 Paperback

New Harbinger Publications' Web site address: www.newharbinger.com

04   03   02

10   9   8   7   6   5   4   3   2   1

First printing

To all the older people among our family, friends and clients, who have enriched our lives and that of our community with their wisdom and experience.

Contents

Preface

For a number of years, we have had the good fortune to work with older adults who have had the courage and commitment to pursue improvement of their mental health and overall well-being. In that time, we have encountered many obstacles that make it difficult for older adults to get the help they need, from such seemingly simple problems as the lack of reliable, affordable transportation to more complex dilemmas including the scarcity of truly accessible mental health services that meet their specific needs.

As part of our jobs, we are constantly thinking, "How can we get services and resources to the people who need them?" Thankfully, there are many other people in our community and across the nation who are asking the same question. Several years ago, we had a talented and curious graduate student working with us who decided to go out to the local bookstore to find a self-help book on depression for the older adults whom we assist. She returned empty-handed, observing that there were many books about how to get over depression, but none that addressed the unique needs of the older adult. "We should write a book!" she said. Thus the seed was planted for this book.

Throughout this book, you will notice our emphasis on the theme that isolation from others impairs your ability to recover from depression. And there's a larger truth here as well: to be removed from society impedes your ability to age successfully, no matter whether you are depressed or not. We repeatedly challenge you, in spite of feeling blue, to reach out and connect with the world around you.

We could not present this idea with such confidence if we did not know of so many older adults who have made this formula work for themselves. We share many personal stories of older adults who have, in spite of depression, found creative and viable ways to increase their activity, form supportive relationships, and feel better as a result. We have taken great care to create the composite characters that you will read about in this book. While details have been fictionalized to protect privacy, the stories are based on the efforts of real people like you. We think that the human spirit and "can-do" attitude of these inspiring people shines through. We have been motivated by how they have overcome depression and we believe that you will also. We recognize that overcoming depression may require more than reading this book and completing the goals, but we believe that it will be a good starting place on your journey of recovery.

We hope that this book will push, nudge, and challenge you to expect more from your life. Our aim is to encourage you to be active, not passive. With the right tools, support, and knowledge, you can take charge of your life in ways you never believed possible. The journey of aging can be challenging enough even in the best of circumstances.

Our goal in writing this book is to help you to strive to bring growth, knowledge, and contentment into each day of your life, and in doing so, make a life-long commitment to your mental and physical well-being.

—Leslie Eckford and Amanda Lambert

Chapter 1

Why Am I So Blue?

Feeling blue from time to time is simply part of being human. When feeling blue becomes depression, it is time to take action. Depression affects people of all ages, but with recognition and appropriate therapies, depression is a treatable condition. Knowing more about it will help you to feel less overwhelmed and more in control of your life. By taking action now, you can get started on the road to recovery.

Joe's Story

"I always felt that if I couldn't take care of myself, I would not want to live. Yet now I can't do anything without help from other people. I have a feeling of emptiness a lot, like there isn't anything there. It's like a big empty hole that can't be filled."

Joe is a seventy-nine-year-old man who experienced significant changes in his life following a heart attack fourteen months ago. He has been restless at night and has difficulty sleeping through the night. He complains of constant fatigue and poor appetite. He has started to have bad feelings about himself, feelings of hopelessness, and even thoughts of suicide. The heart attack and subsequent surgery have left him weak. He is only able to walk with the aid of a walker or a cane and has had to give up most of his activities, including driving and golf. He longs to do the activities that he once enjoyed, and resents being dependent on his wife. He says, "My wife has to help me bathe and makes most of my meals now. I never thought my wife would be taking care of me like this. I feel humiliated and ashamed. I have always taken care of myself." Despite these changes, Joe remains an engaging, pleasant man with a good sense of humor.

Joe went to a doctor, who recommended therapy and started Joe on an anti-depressant medication. Joe participated in group therapy daily for a month and a half. During that time he was able to identify the signs of depression, anxiety, and loss of independence that were impacting his mood and ability to function throughout the day. He was able to express his anger and sadness over losing so much of his ability and having to depend on his wife.

Joe decided to work on some goals, including improving communication with his wife. He encouraged her to allow him to begin to do more things for himself. As Joe became increasingly independent, his self-confidence improved. He set a goal to call friends he had lost touch with; he attended church and made a visit to the local senior center.

Joe also wanted to learn more about changing his attitude. He wrote down positive thoughts whenever negative thoughts cropped up, and he practiced relax-ation techniques three times a week. Slowly, he was able to relax more during the day and sleep better at night. His appetite improved and he no longer had thoughts of suicide and hopelessness. Joe admitted that he still grieved his losses, but accepted his limitations and began to pursue the activities he was still able to do.

Depression and You

Depression is a word that evokes strong emotional and fearful reactions. If you are reading this book, you must be concerned about depression in your life. Some of these reactions are based on fact, but more often they are a result of miscon-ceptions and misinformation not only about mental illness, but about the process of aging as well. Your perceptions about being depressed may come from feel-ings of shame or fear or from the experience of having known someone who was depressed. It may be helpful to honestly ask yourself, "What is my biggest fear about having depression?" Fear generally comes from lack of understanding and accurate information. Fear and lack of information are at the heart of most of the reasons that people don't recognize symptoms of depression and don't seek treat-ment. Some of the fears our clients and their families have expressed about hav-ing depression are listed here:

- **"People will think I can't handle problems on my own."**
  You believe that friends and family members think you are unable to cope

with life, and you yourself have a "bootstrap mentality." You think you should be able to pull yourself up by your bootstraps and get on with life.

- **"Depression will lead to other more serious mental health problems."** You are fearful that having depression will make you susceptible to another mental illness like schizophrenia that is much more serious and difficult to treat.

- **"I am weak and ineffective at managing my own life."** You have managed so far, so why can't you manage your life now? You believe it is because you are a failure in some way or that suddenly your life has taken a turn that you simply can't handle.

- **"My parents didn't raise me right."** You have a vague recollection of information about Freud and the theory that parental guidance has something to do with mental health problems later. You wonder if something went wrong in your childhood that you don't remember.

- **"People will reject me and no one will understand."** You assume that most people will shun you because you have a "mental illness," and you are concerned that some people will be afraid to associate with you.

- **"I will lose my mind and end up in a mental institution."** You are fearful that your depressive state is a precursor of worse things to come. You have an image of what a mental institution is like and may have even known someone who was in one. You believe there is the possibility this will happen to you.

- **"I will never feel any better."** You really do fear that you will always be depressed and that nothing can ever help you to feel better. You can't see any hope for the future.

- **"There is something wrong with my brain that can't be fixed."** You know something is wrong but you don't know exactly what it is or what to do about it. There is a pervasive, intrusive feeling that things are not quite right with the world.

- **"I am getting Alzheimer's disease."** Your symptoms of poor concentration, difficulty attending to people or activity, and memory problems cause you to worry that you may have Alzheimer's disease or some other form of dementia.

Figuring out what your fears are will help to guide you more effectively through the exercises in this book. It's not easy, but once you face your fears, they will no longer have so much influence over you. Depression is not a normal part of aging, but getting older can create an environment of change and transition that may contribute to depression for some people.

We will address the value and importance of exercises and goals in the next chapter. To get you started, however, view the exercises in this chapter as a way of "getting your feet wet." Exercises are simple steps to help you gain a more complete understanding of why you are doing something, because action that is paired with insight will be more meaningful. You'll then move on to goals. Goals require a bit more effort and are designed to move you forward with some action. Goals often involve a change in behavior.

If you find that you are hesitant to write or believe that you are not very good at it, don't worry. Remember that no one is judging you. These exercises and goals are for your benefit. Even if you have physical problems such as arthritis, some limited writing can be very useful as a mental exercise. The very process of thinking and writing is therapeutic. Give it a try! Here is your first exercise.

Exercise: Your Fears About Depression

List some of your fears about having depression here. The more you learn about depression and its treatment, the more comfortable and confident you will begin to feel.

_____

_____

_____

_____

Growing Older: A National Crisis

In a landmark report from the U.S. Surgeon General (Department of Health and Human Services 1999), an exhaustive overview of mental health research concludes: "Our society must resolve to dismantle barriers to seeking help that are sizeable and significant, but not insurmountable." According to this report, most older adults who have depression receive no treatment or inadequate treatment for it. Here are some reasons this topic is important to all of us.

The population in the United States is aging fast. So fast, in fact, that many health-care providers, housing experts, and city planners fear that the nation will be unprepared socially, financially, and psychologically to deal with the vast number of aging individuals and their needs.

The Administration on Aging states that since 1900 the number of Americans sixty-five and older has increased from 3.1 million to 34.5 million. The older population is itself getting older. In 1999 the sixty-five to seventy-four age group was eight times larger than in 1900, the seventy-five to eighty-four age group was sixteen times larger, and the eighty-five and older group was thirty-four times larger.

The older population will continue to expand. The most rapid expansion is expected between the years 2010 and 2030, when the "baby boom" generation reaches sixty-five. By 2030, there will be about 70 million older persons, more than twice their number than in 1999.

You will either benefit or suffer from how our society chooses to manage aging issues. For example, improved longevity increases the chance you will experience geriatric problems such as immobility, memory loss, and other chronic disabilities that could limit your independence. Depression is a chronic disease and has been associated with increased mortality and higher medical costs. The World Health Organization predicts that by the year 2020, the second most disabling disease for the elderly will be depression, surpassed by only heart disease.

Depression can have a dramatic impact on your ability to recover from illnesses and surgery; it can make it more difficult to benefit from rehabilitation regimes such as physical or occupational therapy; it can affect your motivation to stay healthy and take responsibility for your overall well-being. By learning about this treatable condition now, you can begin to take the steps to regain control of your life.

The psychological and emotional needs of older adults have been virtually ignored over the past century. With recognition of the impact the aging population will have on our society, more attention, research, and effort are being directed at understanding what aging is all about. Older people are living longer and increasing in number. The time has come to question traditional assumptions about aging in an effort to extend our lives in a meaningful way that focuses on maintaining independence and physical, mental, and emotional health. We can all benefit from this increased interest in aging, regardless of our life stage.

Attitudes and Aging

"Ageism" is a term that describes discrimination and prejudice against people because of their age—particularly old age. It is a societal concept that guides everything from your attitude about growing older to public policy decisions that are made at the local and national level. Most of us in the United States can't remember the time when older people were revered and venerated for their experience and wisdom. As attitudes have shifted, the focus has been and continues to be on the young. All forms of media from television to print emphasize and glorify the pursuit of youth, which supports a billion-dollar industry devoted to helping people look and act younger. Consequently, old age has been relegated to the bottom of life's totem pole. Even as we make inroads into improving the quality of life for older adults, stereotypes continue to dominate our culture. This attitude is beginning to change, but we still have a long way to go.

This attitude affects not only how other people feel about you, it affects how you feel about yourself. This insidious cycle intrudes into every aspect of your life, from the quality of health care that you receive to public policy. You probably have personal experiences that reflect this attitude that your age makes you less deserving of respect, recognition, and attention.

Exercise: Know Your Own Attitudes

Write five of your negative views on aging.

1. _____

2. _____

3. _____

4. _____

5. _____

List five of your positive views of aging. (If you can think of more, that's great!)

1. _____

2. _____

3. _____

4. _____

5. _____

You may have found it easier to list the negative views than the positive ones. Some of your answers may have revealed some surprising things about your own attitudes. Generally speaking, we are exposed to many more negative or stereotypical views of aging than we are positive, realistic ones.

Challenging the Stereotypes

To some extent, we have been taught and told what to expect at almost every stage of our lives. We know about the characteristics of puberty and adolescence; we have certain expectations of ourselves as we reach adulthood, engage in romantic partnerships, begin families, and build careers. But there is no road map for getting older. No one tells us what to expect, what to look forward to, and how to grow and expand our possibilities. People from all walks of life are beginning to take a more positive, proactive view of aging, and their ideas are beginning to be noticed. If you take the time to seek out these exciting ideas, they may dramatically change the way you think about getting older.

There is a relationship between depression and ageist attitudes. Stereotypical attitudes about aging will affect your perceptions about your mental state. Likewise, many older adults who make complaints of depressive symptoms are often dismissed with comments such as: "Well, you've lived a good life. This is what it's like to get old." Some other stereotypes about aging that are divorced from reality include:

- **Older adults are a burden on society.**
  On the contrary, older adults are productive and contribute millions of dollars to the economy. Many older adults continue to work after "retirement" or contribute valuable volunteer time to their communities. They take care of their grandchildren and their own adult children. It is not uncommon to see three generations living in the same household.

- **Older adults are weak, frail, and disabled.**
  The vast majority of older adults are not frail and disabled. Many are healthy and independent all their lives.

- **Most older adults eventually end up in a nursing home.**
  Only a very small percentage of older adults end up in nursing homes. Most older adults reside in the community and live independently.

- **Once you have reached old age, it is difficult if not impossible to change.**
  Nothing could be further from the truth. Research has shown that older

adults can and do learn new skills, information, and activities their entire lives.

- **Certain medical conditions and physical changes are an inevitable part of getting older and there is no way to prevent these changes.**
  Scientists are proving that the health-related choices that you make can affect whether you will be susceptible to certain diseases. You are never too old to make positive changes that can affect your overall physical health for years to come.

- **Most older adults are unhappy and alone.**
  Most older adults report that they are happy and satisfied with their lives.

- **Older adults are not interested in intimacy or sex.**
  Older adults need sex and intimacy just like younger people. The desire for closeness and physical touch does not go away just because you get older. You are not a different person, just because you are older. You are the same person, with the same needs, likes, dislikes, values, and passions.

"I'm Not Crazy, I Just Feel Bad!"

Many people, when asked what goes through their mind when they hear the word depression, will say, "It means you're crazy." Having depression does *not* mean you are crazy. However, this view directly impacts the ability to recognize true symptoms and to seek the help that is often necessary to treat this illness. The prevailing perspective of mental illness is replete with images of psychotic people corralled in mental institutions—locked up for most of their lives to protect society. For many older adults, admitting that there may be a "mental health" problem is an unimaginable sign of weakness, coming as they do from an era where people took care of their own problems and kept to themselves.

Most older adults have experienced the Great Depression, World War II, and the Korean war. They have raised families and built careers and, in general, have managed quite well. The amazing adaptability of a generation of Americans to a time of uncertainty and sacrifice has not been repeated since. A higher calling to your country demanded that entire families put their personal troubles aside for the greater good. There was a focus on support, camaraderie, and patriotism. No one knew at that time if things would ever improve, or how long the war might last, or whether there would ever be work or enough money. People simply did what they had to do to survive.

One seventy-five-year-old woman puts it this way: "We tend to attribute the effects of the Great Depression and World War II to one generation and in one respect they share this aspect: people felt events were beyond their control. During the depression you did what was necessary to survive a situation you felt wasn't due to your actions. For the most part, war was the same. The difference of course was that we were part of a national effort. It was such a relief to have a cause, which we felt was attainable. Two things bear on this generation's emotional health. One is the feeling, from experience, that some things are out of our control. And the second is that if we are strong enough, we can overcome these things that cause emotional distress. If we don't overcome them, that means we are weak and nothing can help us."

Exercise: Your Unique Challenges

You may not have had this same experience during your life, but take a moment to reflect on your adult years. What were the unique challenges that helped to shape who you are today? Think about your accomplishments and your challenges, both of which contributed to your views today. Don't forget to consider things like: raising a family, starting a new job, going to school, overcoming a physical or emotional challenge, being the best at something, surviving a difficult situation, being helpful to someone else, or giving your time and skill. Write down some of those experiences here.

_____

_____

_____

_____

_____

_____

_____

_____

A New Understanding of Mental Health

In spite of all your achievements, you may feel that the skills that worked then may not be adequate to meet the challenges, changes, and transitions associated with aging now. Things have changed in ways that you may not have been able to anticipate. Expectations are less clear; you may wonder what your purpose is now. Or, perhaps your life today doesn't resemble the one you had envisioned back then. The family is raised, the career is over, people have moved away or passed away, and the country is at peace. What are you supposed to do now? You may have questions about the meaning of life and your place in it and what new skills it will take to age successfully. It may seem inappropriate in some way to talk about these feelings now, considering everything else you have been through.

Certainly much of the information regarding mental health issues is still based on the outdated notion that mental illness is the product of a "bad child-hood" or "poor parenting," but much has changed in the last ten to fifteen years in terms of attitudes regarding mental illness. Notice as you read the ideas below, which are new to you and which ones dispel some of your own misconceptions.

We now know that there is a strong biological and genetic component to mental illness. This does not mean if you have depression that someone else in your family will have it also. It does mean that there is evidence that depression does run in some families. Some families have several members who all have depression.

The treatment of individuals with mental health problems has dramatically improved to include different types of therapies and an emphasis on outpatient treatment. This means that you can get help from seeing a counselor, therapist, or psychiatrist. If you have had chronic depression most of your life, you may remember mental health treatment in the past, or perhaps have been hospitalized. You may have had a bad experience that makes you understandably suspicious of treatment now. Or perhaps you don't have faith in therapy as a way to help you feel better. Being hospitalized for depression is something most people would want to avoid, but in some cases it is necessary to keep someone safe, or to more closely monitor someone's condition. We will talk more about how to find a mental health professional in chapter 10.

Effective and safer medications have been developed, bringing great relief to those suffering from depression. The medications that have been developed for depression over the last several years are very different from the ones you may be familiar with. We will discuss this further in chapter 6.

Individuals with depression are now viewed as having a medical condition much like diabetes or high blood pressure. You wouldn't blame yourself if you were diagnosed with diabetes. You might seek out the expertise of a specialist in the area of diabetes and begin to change your diet and take insulin, if necessary. Depression can be approached with the same perspective.

Juanita's Story

Juanita is a fifty-six-year-old Hispanic woman who was diagnosed with depression by her family physician. She was very reluctant, at first, to discuss with him some of the things she was feeling. Although she managed to take care of her grandkids during the day while her daughter worked, she was neglecting her household duties and sometimes felt too tired to cook dinner for her husband. "I always took pride in keeping my house very clean, and everyone loves my cooking," she said. She began to feel ashamed about not keeping up with the house, and her sunny mood became sad and hopeless. She finally shared her concerns with her doctor, not wanting to tell anyone in the family her troubles.

Juanita's family moved to the United States from Mexico over forty years ago. Here's how she describes her upbringing: "We never talked about depression or anxiety in our family. We were all too busy trying to make ends meet. Depression is something we just don't talk about. We take pride in our strength as a family to come together and overcome adversity. There's no time to be depressed.

"But looking back now, I realize that my mother was depressed too, even though she would never admit it. She was so sad and unhappy most of the time, but I always assumed it was because of our hard life in Mexico and the hope that she always had of a better life for us here in America. She never complained about a thing—she just kept pushing on. I wish she had had the help that I have now. I am seeing a counselor now through Catholic Social Services and have learned that this depression may happen to my children as well. I have concern for them but know now that they can get help if they need it."

Juanita started taking an antidepressant medication and continued therapy for several months. Her mood improved with time and she resumed many of the activities that she had dropped. Although Juanita's condition improved dramatically, she still struggled from time to time over the years with depressive episodes, but didn't hesitate to call her counselor when this occurred. She also made certain to let her family know when she felt she needed some extra support and help.

Depression Is a Whole-Body Illness

We have come a long way in understanding the causes and treatment of depression. Depression is a medical condition associated with changes in brain chemistry as well as the body's response to stress. It is a condition that affects emotions, feelings, thinking, and perceptions as well as physical health. Although we will be covering the symptoms of depression more fully later in this chapter, we will start with some of the ways in which depression is considered to be a holistic illness that can affect every system of your body, including the brain.

- **Emotions:** You may have periods of uncontrollable crying for no apparent reason. You may feel lost, confused, sad, angry, irritable, lonely, or afraid. You may feel as though you are just "not yourself." Your emotions are on the surface and hard to control.

- **Thinking:** Your thinking may be confused, unclear, or distracted. You may have problems concentrating or attending to the simplest tasks. Situations that once seemed effortless may now seem insurmountable.

- **Body:** Depression can affect the body in countless ways. You may have aches and pain "all over," or problems with sleep, appetite, digestion, or energy. You may have headaches, backaches, or other muscle tension.

- **Attitude:** Your attitude is a reflection of how you are relating to the world and the people in it. Depression may distort your view of the world in such a way that things just don't seem quite "right." The world may seem different to you than it ever has before. Your optimism is replaced with pessimism and negative thinking; other people you know may seem "odd" or not themselves. Activities that once were enjoyable now seem lifeless and unimportant. Or perhaps your perceptions are so distorted that you don't have a realistic view of how bad things really are. You may need to rely on other people close to you who can more accurately tell you about your attitude.

Exercise: How Depression Affects You

Think about all the ways depression affects you as a whole and integrated being. Identifying these now will help you with goals in later chapters.

Emotions: _____

_____

Thinking: _____

_____

Body: _____

_____

Attitude: _____

_____

After completing this exercise, you may be saying to yourself, "I'm a wreck!" Give yourself credit for having the courage to take an honest look at how you are being affected by depression. Becoming more aware of these changes now will give you a better perspective on how much you will improve later.

"I Hope I'm Not Alone"

Depression is one of the most common mental health problems. According to the National Institute of Mental Health, it is estimated that in any given one-year period, 9.5 percent of the population, or about 18.8 million American adults, will suffer from a depressive illness. Great strides have been made in the treatment and understanding of depression in children, adolescents, and adults. However, information on the frequency, causes, symptoms, and treatment of depression in older adults is not as well understood. People are just beginning to talk seriously about depression and older adults. Estimates do vary, but according to the Department of Health and Human Services, a very small percentage of older adults—less than 3 percent—report seeing mental health specialists for treatment of depression. Many primary care physicians do not recognize the symptoms of depression in older adults and may not ask their patients the questions that will help them make the correct diagnosis. You may have had the experience of trying to express to your doctor what you are feeling, only to be dismissed or not taken seriously enough. Fortunately, many doctors are beginning to change their attitudes toward their older patients.

Estimates vary widely on the occurrence of depression in older adults for several important reasons:

The Stigma of Mental Illness

We talked about this earlier, but it is not uncommon for older adults considering mental health treatment to be afraid of being involuntarily hospitalized. It is important to realize that this only occurs when someone is severely ill. In the past you may have heard stories about a relative who had a "nervous breakdown" and wasn't seen for a long time. You may harbor fears about mental hospitals or institutions. Today, involuntary commitments are infrequent and occur only during very severe forms of illness.

A Reluctance to Talk About Personal Problems

It may be uncomfortable for you to talk about your feelings. Generally speaking, a generation that endured war and the Great Depression put other concerns aside. Perhaps you believe that expressing feelings is inappropriate, shameful, or a sign of weakness. You don't want to burden other people with your problems.

Misattribution of Depression Symptoms to "Normal Aging"

You may presume that as you age, you should expect to feel tired, unmotivated, and less enthusiastic about life. If you knew a thirty-year-old who felt this way, would you consider it normal? A significant change in the way you feel and function is cause for concern, regardless of your age.

A Missed Diagnosis or Misdiagnosis

Many well-intentioned and harried health-care providers may attribute your depressive symptoms to other illnesses. For example, if you have a heart condition, a health-care provider may assume that your symptoms of fatigue, poor sleep, and loss of appetite are due to the medical condition that brought you in for treatment.

A Different Presentation of Symptoms

Many older adults do not use the word "depression" or even necessarily feel depressed. Moreover, depressive symptoms may appear differently in older people than in other age groups. Cultural differences may dictate the way and manner in which depression is expressed. We will talk more about this later.

When Depression Turns Deadly

Suicide is something some people would rather not talk about. Out of respect to family members, many deaths are not identified publicly as suicides. There are religious considerations and feelings of shame and anger. But the facts indicate a pressing need to increase awareness of this tragic problem. There is an important distinction between having thoughts of suicide because you are depressed compared to considering ending your life because of a terminal illness. According to the Surgeon General's Report (Department of Health and Human Services 1999):

- Older persons (sixty-five years of age and older) have the highest suicide rates of any age group.

- The suicide rate among men eighty-five years and older is twice the rate of the general population, especially if there is a history of alcohol use.

- Suicide in older adults is most often associated with late-onset depression: among patients seventy-five years of age and older, 60 to 75 percent of suicides have diagnosable depression.

- In a study of ninety-seven adults aged fifty years and older who committed suicide, fifty-one had seen their primary care physician within one month of the suicide.

All but a few adults who commit suicide are suffering from depression. If you or someone you know is suicidal, contact your doctor or a mental health professional immediately. Remember that depression is a treatable medical condition and thoughts of suicide are a symptom of depression. It is widely accepted that a combination of medication and therapy is the most effective treatment for older adults. Both of these topics will be covered in more detail in other chapters.

The Price of Undiagnosed Depression

The costs associated with undiagnosed depression are staggering. They include: increased hospitalization, prolonged rehabilitation and nursing home care, increased disability, intensified pain and other medical symptoms, problems with memory, confusion, and concentration, and of course suicide. Imagine that you are hospitalized for hip replacement surgery or some other major medical condition. You wake up from surgery in a hospital bed all alone, and it begins to dawn on you that your life has changed in dramatic ways. All of the basic activities you used to do on your own, like going to the bathroom or getting a drink of water, are a challenge now. You know that the surgery was necessary to relieve your pain and will eventually help with your mobility, but in the meantime, someone will need to help you with almost everything you do. You feel lonely and afraid. Consider the effect of having depression in addition to your other medical problems in this scenario. Your ability and willingness to participate in and benefit from the recovery process would be greatly affected.

According to the Surgeon General's report, up to 63 percent of adults aged sixty-five and older have mental health needs that go unmet. The most serious consequence of untreated depression is increased mortality from suicide or other illnesses associated with depression. Depression for all age groups is one of the most costly diseases in the United States, estimated to cost approximately $43 billion a year. Older adults with depression visit the doctor and emergency room more often, use more medication, do not adhere as well to rehabilitation regimes, and stay longer in the hospital. We will discuss depression and medical conditions in chapter 9.

Other less tangible but equally significant factors are the costs associated with quality of life. You may already recognize how dramatically your life has been altered by depression. Untreated depression impairs your ability to enjoy life and places a strain on family and friends who often do not know how to help. Or perhaps you are suffering without really understanding why and find it difficult to be around other people because you know something is wrong. It can cause months or even years of needless suffering that take a financial and emotional toll on families, communities, and health-care systems.

The Warning Signs to Look For

You need to know what the symptoms of depression are before you can know whether you or someone else has it. The very word "depression" harbors such negative connotations that some older adults will go to extreme lengths to deny any symptoms that may be associated with it. A diagnosis of depression is made by qualified health-care professionals based on criteria developed by the American Psychiatric Association in the *Diagnostic and Statistical Manual of Mental Disorders* (DSM-IV-TR 2000). This manual describes symptoms for all types of mental and depressive disorders.

You may have had a history of depression dating back many years, and as you got older you experienced a recurrence of this depression. Or you may have never had an episode of depression until late in life. It is also possible that you believe you are having your first episode of depression but actually have experienced a minor depression earlier that was overlooked or has been forgotten.

Although the symptoms listed here are generally accepted as being true for most people, you are a unique person with your own particular experiences and feelings. Human behavior and emotions can't be condensed into a simple checklist, but a guide will make it easier for you to recognize the areas of your life that are affected by depression.

Read the following symptoms carefully and check the ones that you think apply to you:

☐ **Depressed mood, or feeling "down in the dumps."**

☐ **Loss of interest in activities you used to enjoy.**

☐ **Significant weight loss or weight gain:** Have you been eating more or less than usual? Some people think eating one meal a day is normal in old age. Losing or gaining weight unintentionally is an indication that eating patterns have changed. See chapter 8 for more discussion on the topic of nutrition.

☐ **Difficulty sleeping or sleeping too much:** Do you toss and turn at bedtime or do you awaken during the night and have trouble returning to sleep? Or do you struggle to get out of bed in the morning and/or stay in your pajamas during the day?

☐ **Restlessness:** Do you pace around the house or have difficulty sitting still? Do you have a strange, unidentifiable restlessness (sometimes even in spite of fatigue) that isn't satisfied with normal activity?

☐ **Fatigue or loss of energy:** Do you feel tired during the day? Do routine activities just wear you out? Are you fatigued even after lots of sleep?

☐ **Feelings of worthlessness or excessive guilt:** Do you find yourself worrying about things that happened years ago, or about things that you have no control over? Have you lost your self-confidence?

☐ **Difficulty concentrating, or indecisiveness:** Have you been more forgetful lately? Do you have difficulty making even the easiest decisions?

☐ **Recurrent thoughts of death, or recurrent suicidal thoughts:** Do you sometimes feel like it would be better if you didn't wake up the morning, or that everyone would be better off without you? Do you think about ending your life?

☐ **Frequent crying:** Do you find yourself in tears for no apparent reason? Or, do you feel like crying, but no tears come?

☐ **Physical complaints with no identifiable cause:** Are you more aware of aches and pains? Perhaps your stomach is upset or you have headaches. If you have pain from some medical problem, depression may make the pain feel worse than usual.

☐ **Complaints of poor memory:** Is it difficult for you to concentrate or attend to everyday activities? Do you find yourself trying to read something only to discover you are at the end of the page and don't recall what you read? You may feel very distracted and unable to focus on things that ordinarily are very interesting and stimulating for you.

☐ **Pessimism:** Do others comment on your "bad attitude"? Are you more irritable than usual? Do you resent other people's apparent happiness? You have no real hope that you will ever feel better. The world seems like a bitter and hostile place.

☐ **Excessive negative thoughts:** Do you worry about things that are out of your control? Do you assume the worst? Do you have recurrent bad thoughts about yourself? You can't seem to remember a time when you felt good about yourself.

☐ **Anxiety:** Is it difficult for you to stop worrying once you get started? Are you uncharacteristically nervous around other people or reluctant to leave the house? (See chapter 7.)

To be on the safe side, if you have checked three or more of the above symptoms, contact a qualified mental health professional who can do a more complete evaluation to determine whether you do have clinical depression.

Depression by Any Other Name

There are other disorders that have depression as a prominent feature. The three we are going to briefly discuss here are *dysthymia, bipolar disorder,* and *seasonal affective disorder*.

Dysthymia

The National Mental Health Association describes dysthymia as a disorder with somewhat milder symptoms than the major depression we have been talking about. It is a very common type of depression that differs from major depression in symptom duration. People with dysthymia experience a chronically depressed mood that occurs for most of the day more days than not for at least two years.

The warning signs of dysthymia are:

• Poor school/work performance

• Social withdrawal

• Shyness

• Irritable hostility

- Conflicts with family and friends

- Physiological abnormalities

- Sleep irregularities

- Parents with major depression

If you have never had a major depressive episode but have the symptoms of dysthymia, you are at risk for developing a major depressive episode over the next year.

Many of the symptoms listed above are the same as those for depression. The main difference is the length of time these symptoms last. With dysthymia the symptoms last at least two years, and with depression, the symptoms are present for a minimum of two weeks. Because people with dysthymia often have only two or three of the symptoms associated with major depression, it is often overlooked (Jacobs 2000).

Bipolar Disorder

Everyone experiences mood changes. But the extreme highs and lows of bipolar disorder are not normal. Bipolar disorder is a disorder that is characterized by periods of mania and depression. These mood swings can last for days, weeks, or even months. In the depressed stage, people experience all of the typical symptoms of depression that we have talked about. The manic phase consists of the following symptoms, which we will not go into in detail. Please refer to the suggested readings in the Resources section to get more information on bipolar disorder.

- Heightened mood, exaggerated optimism and self-confidence

- Decreased need for sleep without fatigue

- Grandiose delusions, inflated sense of self-importance

- Excessive irritability, aggressive behavior

- Increased physical, mental activity

- Racing speech, flight of ideas, impulsiveness

- Poor judgment, easily distracted

- Reckless behavior such as spending sprees, rash business decisions, erratic driving, sexual indiscretions

- In the most severe cases, auditory hallucinations

(Used with permission of the National Depressive and Manic-Depressive Association 1998)

There is a very strong genetic susceptibility to bipolar disorder. The illness tends to run in families, and close relatives of someone with bipolar disorder are more likely to be affected by the disorder (National Alliance for the Mentally Ill 2001). If you recognize these symptoms in yourself, you may have bipolar disorder, and it is important for you to see a mental health professional who can initiate the appropriate medication.

Seasonal Affective Disorder

Seasonal affective disorder (SAD) is a type of mood fluctuation that follows the seasons, with depressive symptoms occurring in the winter months. In the spring and summer, the depression lifts, and normal or even elevated mood returns. Current research indicates that lack of sunlight may lead to the symptoms of SAD. The typical symptoms of depression that occur in the winter months include loss of energy, decreased activity, slowed thinking, sadness, and often excessive eating and sleeping. SAD is different from the "holiday blues," which also occur in the winter months as a result of stress associated with the holiday season. The most common treatment of SAD is exposure to intense light for a period of time each day. Antidepressant medications and therapy are also helpful.

"Why Is This Happening to Me?"

There is not one single, definitive cause of depression. Many things can contribute to depression, and in some cases people become depressed for no apparent reason. Some of you may be able to identify a depression "trigger." Others of you may have no idea why this is happening to you. Here are some of the factors that have been identified as being associated with depression:

- People with depression typically have too little or too much of certain brain chemicals called *neurotransmitters*. Changes in these chemicals can cause or contribute to depression. The primary neurotransmitter that you may have heard of is *serotonin*. There is some evidence to suggest that age, gender, and hormonal changes affect these chemicals. You cannot take a pill that supplies more of these neurotransmitters, but you can take medication that affects the action of these brain chemicals, thereby improving your mood. (See chapter 6.)

- Depression is more likely to occur in conjunction with certain illnesses such as stroke, heart disease, cancer, Parkinson's disease, diabetes, chronic pain, and hormonal problems. However, this does not mean that if you have one of these diseases you will necessarily get depression.

- Some prescription medications have symptoms of depression as a side effect. Have your doctor or your pharmacist evaluate all your medications to see if one or more may be the culprit.

- Difficult life events, losses, and transitions can contribute to depression. Examples of these would be: losing a loved one, moving to a new place, developing medical problems, losing the ability to drive, becoming immobilized, or being isolated from friends and family. For example, Margie loses her son to Hodgkin's disease and says, "I never thought I'd outlive my kids." Frank's children pressure him to move out of his home of twenty-five years into an assisted living facility. He states: "I should never have left my home until I was ready."

- Heredity can also play a part in the development of depression. A family history of depression may make it more likely for you to have depression. There are research studies that follow family histories to establish a genetic link for depression.

- Alcohol abuse or prescription medication abuse can contribute to or complicate depression. Alcohol is a depressant, and the abuse of alcohol can exacerbate or contribute to a depression.

The above can be causes for depression in any age group. As an older adult you may differ from younger age groups in the following ways:

- You may not have as much social support now that your children have moved away or are too busy to spend much time with you. When you were younger you probably had a busy life with friends from work, church, synagogue, and neighborhood. Social connections change as you age. This is something we will talk about in detail in chapter 3.

- You may have medical problems and financial constraints. Of course, these may have been problems when you were younger as well, but getting older does increase your risk of getting certain age-related illnesses. Physical health is the foundation of independent functioning. After retirement you may be on a fixed income that places some constraints on your activities.

- You may have difficulty in accessing care. Accessing care means finding a therapist or counselor and being able to pay for it. It could mean finding reliable, affordable transportation or knowing where to go for help. You may live in a rural community that has limited mental health resources.

- You may have had other stresses in your life such as moving from your home, losing a spouse or partner, or having to take care of a family member with a chronic illness. Many older adults end up having grown children live with them and in some cases three generations live in the same house.

Although these are not necessarily causes of depression, they can be contributing and complicating factors.

Depression is an illness we know much about, but we still have much to learn. Recognizing your symptoms, understanding the importance of treatment, and not being afraid to ask for help are vital steps on the road to recovery. You may be feeling overwhelmed right now, but by reading this book and working on the exercises and goals, you are making the choice to gain control of your life. We have seen many older adults do it, and we know you can do it too!

Chapter 2

Your First Steps
to Recovery

Goal setting may sound deceptively easy. But people with depression lose motivation and energy, and often along with this, the ability to plan effectively. Setting goals provides direction and focus. When you follow through on a goal, you will have a sense of accomplishment.

Annette's Story

Annette was no stranger to work and accomplishments. She and her husband Frank had raised three children while Annette worked as a legal secretary at a busy law firm. There were plenty of times when they had had to struggle financially, and they also dealt with the challenges of having a child with developmental problems. Annette gave a lot of credit to her marriage as a source of her strength during those years. "It was never easy, but we had each other and we were a good team."

Now Frank was ill with advanced Parkinson's disease and Annette could not rely on him as she had in the past. She felt in some ways that he had already left her and she debated making a decision to sell the home that they had worked so hard for. She hated the idea of moving into a retirement condominium.

"Suddenly, it seemed like I couldn't think straight. All that was on my mind was how I could make this decision. I thought I would go crazy. I'd never had a problem making my mind up about anything before." Annette felt anxious and worried a lot about things that had never bothered her before. She felt sad and hopeless and avoided seeing her friends, making excuses to stay at home. "It just made me too sad to go anywhere without Frank."

Annette finally sought help through a counselor. The counselor suggested that Annette start by setting some simple goals to help her improve her mood and thinking. Annette bristled at the idea of setting goals. As a capable woman of seventy-three, she resented the very notion that she needed to set "baby steps" to help her get better. "I felt like I was a school child, that I was having to do homework again." But she felt even more frustrated that she wasn't going out and doing things, and realized that she had to start somewhere.

At first, with the counselor's advice, Annette made her goals very small and simple, something that she could practice for a few minutes each day, such as eating a healthy breakfast each morning and taking a five-minute walk. "It seemed so basic. But as I started to pay attention to what I was eating, I felt that I could do something about it." The next week, Annette started practicing some deep breathing exercises to help her feel more at ease. "At first I really had to think about this. I hadn't realized that when I was worrying, my breathing was getting faster and more shallow. After I started practicing deep breathing, I felt more in control." Eventually she built up to making an appointment with her financial advisor and getting more information about selling her home. "It surprised me. I hadn't realized how poor my attention had been. Even though my first goals were things that I knew how to do, it really helped me to focus on them. I started to feel like I was getting things accomplished and I started feeling better."

First Steps First

One of the most important elements in the process of healing from a depressed mood is to change your thinking and behavior. When you are depressed, your thoughts tend to be so negative that it makes doing normal activities almost impossible. Depression makes you feel stuck in a downward spiral with little hope of returning to health. You feel like you are in a black hole and do not know how to get out.

Setting and working on goals is an essential tool for combating depression and the unhealthy behaviors that accompany it. Many studies have shown that by making simple changes in behavior, your attitude and thoughts can become more positive and productive. We have seen many older people with depression use this concept with great success. Even people with very poor energy and motivation can begin to recover when they start making and working on goals.

How to Do the Exercises and Goals in This Book

In this and the following chapters, we will discuss goals and exercises that you can work on to speed your recovery from depression. The exercises are questions and ideas for you to consider and write down as you are reading each chapter. Simply write down your immediate thoughts; don't spend a lot of time on them. The goals, on the other hand, are more like homework that you may spend more time on. The goals usually require some activity or practice outside of the time that you are reading the book.

Goals: The Steps to a Productive Life

Consciously or not, you have probably been doing some sort of goal planning most of your life. You may have achieved some small successes merely by lucky breaks or good timing, but a game plan of some type is usually required. For example, think of when you got your first job as an adult. Maybe it was when you were just out of school or before you married or after you were discharged from the service. You had to start with some idea of where you would go to get a job, and whom you would ask. You may have written out a list of potential employers. Perhaps you thought about your skills and practiced your typing in order to do your best. You may have even been a bit nervous and had to find some way of building up your nerve to "hit the pavement." You probably thought about what you would wear to meet an employer and got your clothes out the night before to press them so you'd look as sharp as possible. There were probably these and at least a few other steps to getting a job. In other words, it took some thought, planning and action.

As you get older, you may think that it is not important to plan and make goals. Without the emphasis on career or the structure of certain roles in your life, you might decide that it is not necessary. This disconnects you from a sense of responsibility and direction. It can be destructive to your self-esteem, and may leave you feeling less in control of your life and more uncertain. Strengthening your skills in goal planning at this time of your life can have many benefits.

Characteristics of Goals

In order to recover from depression, you will need a plan of action, and your goals will be the foundation of that plan. Establishing and working on goals will allow you to take a proactive stance in improving your health. Keep in mind that:

- There are long-term goals and short-term goals.

- The long-term goal is to decrease the symptoms of depression, return to feeling more like your "old self," and be actively engaged and satisfied in life.

- Having short-term goals will help you get to your long-term goal. Think of short-term goals as the building blocks for long-term goals.

- The short-term goals will be just that: things that you can do in small steps over short periods of time, such as a week.

- Having goals and following through with them can help you maintain control over your own life and have greater independence. When you make the decisions and follow through with a plan on your own, you are the captain of your ship.

- The goals will be worthless unless you decide to do them and take action.

Recovery from depression will not happen overnight. The length of time it takes is highly variable among individuals. You will probably find that this is a process that has its own ups and downs. Beginning the course of recovery from depression is something like being on the first rung of a ladder. Getting started in therapy or self-help can offer some initial relief and increased hopefulness to some depressed people. You climb up two rungs of the ladder. As you continue to face your fears and concerns, however, you sometimes hit a plateau or even experience a lower mood. You slip down three rungs. This can be discouraging. Fortunately, it is usually temporary, and as you have the chance to work through your doubts and find solutions, you make greater strides. Then you climb more confidently to the top. The depression begins to lift and you feel more able to do the things that you want to do. It is more realistic for you to expect this type of progression than a swift ascent up the ladder.

Goals are the rungs of the ladder that one climbs to get to the top. You will build your ladder with smaller, short-term goals first. Some of the goals may seem silly to you. We will ask you to do some things that you should be doing every day to take care of yourself. Other goals may be activities that you are not familiar with, and these may be uncomfortable or seem a bother. Setting goals will help you practice successful strategies for recovery so you will begin to feel better.

Exercise: Prioritize Your Goals

Look back at the symptoms of depression that you checked on the list in chapter 1. Identify which are the worst two in your view and write them down here:

1. _____

2. _____

Your first goals will address these symptoms.

"But I Can't Think Straight"

Remember that the purpose of establishing and completing goals is to increase your focus on what you want in your life. This will help improve your concentration. Depression may cause forgetfulness, confusion, and difficulty concentrating. This can be particularly distressing. Naturally, you would be concerned about something like Alzheimer's developing. Certainly there are some mild changes that occur in your memory as you age. These are normal and you may experience what many people call "senior moments."

People of any age with depression, however, tend to be so distracted by their negative thoughts that they do not pay attention as much as they need to and thus do not remember things. But we have found repeatedly that if depression is treated and you focus on the steps of recovery, thinking and memory can improve. It only makes sense that if you become more conscientious about what you are doing and what you are thinking each day, your concentration will get stronger.

Exercise: Memory Checkup

Have you had more forgetful moments than usual lately? For example, you may find that when reading a book, you get to the end of the page and cannot remember what it was about. You may walk into a room and not remember why you went there. Write down your concerns about your memory or concentration here. Share these concerns with your family and doctor.

_____

_____

_____

_____

"What Good Will It Do Me?"

You may find yourself resisting the idea of setting goals. Give yourself a chance to try them before rejecting the idea. Remember, you are being influenced by powerful negative feelings, such as hopelessness and helplessness, that accompany depression. Don't let those feelings make important decisions for you.

We often encounter people who are looking for the "magic pill" or for someone or something outside of themselves to "fix" things so that they will feel less depressed. You should investigate if you have succumbed to any of these self-defeating tendencies. Watch out for the following pitfalls:

- You may say things like "I would be fine if my (spouse, adult child) would just start doing more to help me around the house."

- "If my doctor would just find the right medication for me, I would feel better."

- You have suffered for a long time and are convinced that "nothing can help." In some respects, you take on the symptoms of depression as part of your personality and lose touch with your real self. You may feel bitter and rejected.

- You try a few things now and then to see if you can feel better, but give up after a few days because "it didn't work."

- When someone makes suggestions that might help but require your effort, you respond by saying "*Yes, but* that won't work because . . ." You have an abundant supply of reasons and rationalizations to explain why nothing will change anything.

Even if your own reasons for feeling helpless may sound accurate on the surface, they are not necessarily true. And saying no to all your options *definitely* results in less hope for improvement. Have you said things like the comments above to yourself or to others who have tried to help you? If so, you may be closing the door to anything ever helping you. This is a choice that you may be making without being aware of it.

Exercise: "Yes, But . . ."

Write down any "*Yes, but . . .*" or "*It won't work because . . .*" statements that you may have said or thought when others made suggestions to you or in response to ideas in this book. Be honest!

_____

_____

_____

Get the Most Out of Your Goals

In order for this book to help you, you must put away your doubts. Just reading this book isn't enough—you must do the steps and be involved. It won't be easy. You'll need to:

- Push yourself and be willing to give up your "comfort zone" at times. That means doing some things that you may not want to do.

- Dare to think differently about things in your life.

- Take some risks. This may feel ridiculous, tiresome, boring, or even weird at times. But what matters is how you feel after you make the effort.

- Do things all the way, not halfway. You won't know if something will work until you try it. That means that you *really* try it, not just think about it, or say you are going to do it, or only do it for five minutes.

- This does not require perfection, but a willingness to try.

- Timing is everything. If you think as you are reading this that this sounds like something that you cannot or will not do, then this may not be the right time for you to set to work on this. But if your response is "I'll do whatever it takes to feel more like myself again," then it's probably a great time for you to get started.

- Unless you are willing to be an active participant, recovery is unlikely.

Esther's Story

Esther, a seventy-five-year-old woman, had been through many difficult experiences in her life. After growing up on a farm during the Depression, she married with the hope of raising a family of her own. She looked forward to giving her children the love and attention that she felt she had not received from her own parents. Her husband, however, did not help Esther realize that dream. He was abusive to Esther and their children. Eventually, she left the marriage and became a single working mother. "Times were hard. I worked every kind of job that I could. I waited tables, I worked at the plant, whatever I could get. I did what I had to do and we were always just scraping by." She was proud of herself for taking care of her children and being a hard worker. She had a close relationship with her children and felt good about how she had raised them.

A few years ago, Esther's oldest son was killed in a car accident. "I really didn't know how I could live after I lost Raymond. He was such a special boy." Esther went into an emotional tailspin. She became very depressed and worried about her other children constantly. She became fearful about going anywhere and declined offers to be involved with her family or friends. She spent most of her time alone in her apartment. Her grief and anger about her son's death turned to bitterness. "I felt that there was little use in trying to do anything right anymore. What would be the point? Life will take it out of you no matter what you do."

Esther's doctor tried to talk to her about depression. She was skeptical that anything could help her feel better. She was scared to even take an aspirin and when the doctor suggested an antidepressant, Esther was certain that it would make her feel worse. She would try a medication for a day or two and decide that she felt too sick to take it anymore. "It didn't help anyway." She didn't even bother to tell the doctor that she was not taking the medication.

A nurse who lived down the street from Esther urged her to go to a therapist. Just to show her friend that it was pointless, Esther made an appointment with the therapist. "When I went there, I had it in my mind that it would be the only time. But for some reason, I decided to go back." Esther talked to the therapist about how depressed she was feeling, and about the pain that she felt about her son's death. "But when she started to suggest things for me to do, I felt angry. She must not have understood how much pain I was in. I was so certain that there was no solution." On the surface, Esther would agree to try some self-help activities that her therapist suggested. But when she got home, she would convince herself that it would be a waste of her time. "I even thought that it could make me feel worse."

When Esther did not make any progress, her therapist talked to her about her resistance. She pointed out to Esther how some of her behavior was holding her back from getting better. She assured Esther that this tendency to resist is not unusual, and that it's important to understand it and learn how to deal with it. Esther went home and thought about it. "I knew she was right. I realized that my pain had been my companion for a long time. It was familiar. It had become hard to imagine living without it. But I also realized that part of me was ready to let it go."

With the help of the therapist and the support of her friend, Esther began a slow process of doing self-help activities and working on goals. She had to actively challenge herself when she began to question in her mind if anything would help. Esther agreed to go back to her doctor and try a different medication to help with her efforts. She took the pills each day as directed by her doctor. Over time, she began to feel more comfortable going out of her apartment. She reconnected with her family and had more confidence in their safety. Her grieving for her son became less intense. "I realized that it would be all right if I did not think about Raymond every moment. It would not mean that I loved him or missed him any less. It would just be different."

Why You Need a Coach

Although you are the most important person involved in overcoming your depression, it does not mean that you should go it alone. In fact, it is our experience that you will have a much more successful recovery from depression when you have some organized, planned support from others. If you don't talk to others about the depression, it makes it easy for you to deny its intensity and its meaning in your life. And if you don't get a chance to hear another person's perspective, you may also be more likely to blame yourself unrealistically for your symptoms.

We suggest that you select a "coach." It may be more than one person. Your coach should be someone who:

- is not expected to do the work for you, but rather will be there to help guide you and cheer for you as you progress

- you know and trust to talk with about your thoughts and feelings and with whom you can bounce ideas around

- will sometimes remind you to do your goals and help you think of new ones

- has your best interests at heart

As you are reading this, you may be thinking to yourself, "But I don't want to bother anyone else with my problems." Even if you are not the type to share your intimate thoughts with someone else, it is critical to give it a try if you want to get out of feeling depressed. One of the most insidious features of depression is its tendency to make you withdraw from other people. You begin to doubt that people will care, or you feel like they will think you are crazy. Slowly but surely, you talk less to people that you know and you become even less likely to get to know new people. You may even find that it is harder to talk, that you do not express your ideas very well because you are out of practice.

But talking helps. Problems often seem bigger in our heads than they really are. One way to find this out is to let yourself "think out loud" by speaking about what is on your mind. As you talk and exchange ideas, your mind is stimulated. Thinking can get clearer. For some, this first step can bring a lot of relief. It's good to hear how another person may react to your problems, and that person may even offer a new perspective that had not occurred to you. They may think of solutions that may have seemed impossible to you until you heard it from their angle. And most importantly, you can feel their support.

You may say, "I've been talking about this for years and it doesn't help!" Perhaps you have been talking, but without a clear direction or purpose. You may have given a litany of your symptoms over and over. In your own mind or in your family's opinion, you may seem like a complainer. You may be feeling so bad that it has been hard to think about anything else. You may be tired of talking because you sound like a broken record. Or, you may think that you have been talking but really have expected others to read your mind and understand how miserable you are feeling. You may even have been going to a therapist or a psychiatrist and find that you feel stuck and are not making any progress. If any of these possibilities are true, then you need to find a new way of expressing yourself and working on solutions. And you will want to become clear about the purpose and the result that you want from talking. Having a coach will help you stay on track.

How do you choose your coach? It should be someone you know and trust. You may need more than one person; the more support you have from other people, the better. You will need to meet or have phone contact with your coach on at least a weekly basis while your symptoms are at their most intense. Here are some ideas of who this person or persons could be:

- **A friend or a family member.** People who know you well and care about you may feel good about doing something positive to help you feel better.

- **Someone whom you have met at a support group.** Perhaps you have attended a group for people with depression or grieving and loss. There is probably someone whom you felt a connection to and they would have the experience to understand what you are going through. You could even be their coach in time!

- **Someone from your local Aging Services agency.** Many such agencies have Senior Companion-type programs that arrange for a person to come and visit you regularly in your home. This person may be ideal for your coach.

- **A case manager.** If you are receiving any type of social services you may have a case manager who may be willing to help by being your coach.

- **A neighbor.** Many people complain these days that they don't get a chance to know their neighbors in the way that they used to. You may have some positive feelings about a neighbor but have not invested much in the relationship. At the same time, we frequently hear that neighbors do offer to help, but a depressed person tends to turn this help away. Your neighbors may be glad to assist.

- **Someone from a cultural, religious, or activity group that you belong to.** Many people who belong to such groups do so because they want to be more connected to other people. Some of these groups may have volunteers who particularly want to help older adults who need help. Think about friends that you have made over the years in a drawing class, a community service group, a garden club, a church group, or a cultural heritage group. A good candidate for a coach may be among them, even if you have not seen them for a while.

- **Think intergenerationally.** We have heard from some older adults with depression that the person who is most supportive to them in terms of their depression is someone younger than themselves. Examples are a nephew or a granddaughter, a young neighbor who is a stay-at-home mom, or a younger person whom you mentored at work. Younger people often have a broader experience with talking about feelings and can be more sympathetic.

In any case, your coach should be someone who has a basic understanding of depression and who will not judge you for having it. You could share with them the information about depression in chapter 1 of this book. It helps if the person will understand your ups and downs in the process of recovery, but will not hesitate to remind you when you are not doing what you set out to do.

If you have been seeing a therapist, you may wonder if the therapist is currently acting as your coach or could fill that role in the future. It depends on your therapist, so this is something that you could discuss with them. Every therapist has their own view of therapy and what it will include. However, if you present them with the goals that you are working on, they may welcome hearing how you are progressing and devote time in your session to reviewing your goals with you. At the same time, your therapist may believe that it would be more helpful to you to have someone else be your coach and thereby expand the number of supports that you have.

Rex's Story

Rex has always considered himself a loner. At eighty-three, he has never been married and lives in his own home. He and his brother owned and operated a janitorial service. He was very actively involved in all phases of the business, from keeping the books to going out on a job to clean an office building. He enjoyed his work and got along well with his brother. When his brother decided to retire about ten years ago and gave his half of the business to his son, Rex's nephew, Bob, Rex continued working. "The business was my life," he says. Over the past few years, though, Rex felt pressure from Bob to retire. "Maybe I wasn't as fast as I used to be. But I know that I was doing the work just fine. Maybe he just wanted me out of his way. I felt I was just old wood being thrown out." Over time, he became depressed and retreated into his retirement. Rex stopped going out to the park for a daily walk. He began to watch more television, even though "there isn't much worth watching." His house became more disorganized and he had trouble finding things. "I really began to wonder why I was still around, just taking up space. I felt pretty hopeless."

When Rex recognized that something was wrong, he asked his doctor to help. The doctor recommended group therapy, so Rex joined a group of other older adults coping with depression. It was suggested to Rex that he get a coach in his life to aid his recovery. "I remember thinking, 'How am I going to do that?' I really am not that close to anyone." So Rex asked for advice from other people in the group who had already found a coach. Rex started by listing all the people that he could think of who had been helpful to him over the years. He wondered if his niece Jenny might be able to help him. "She has always been my favorite and she takes the time to call me." Rex talked to the group about his misgivings about asking Jenny for help. "She's got too much on her plate as it is, taking care of her own family." They pointed out that Jenny already showed Rex that she cares about him. They also asked Rex about what he might have done for Jenny during her life. Rex thought of the times that Jenny had talked to him about problems she was having at work, and those occasions when she had needed help with her garden and Rex had pitched in. He realized that it would be worth a try.

When Rex talked to Jenny about being his coach, he was surprised and relieved that she readily agreed. In fact, Jenny told Rex that she had noticed a change in him since he had gotten depressed but was unsure of how to approach him about it. Jenny had always admired her Uncle Rex and didn't want to offend him if she was wrong about his feelings. She let Rex know that she was eager to help him get better.

Rex and Jenny agreed to meet on Saturday. They went over the symptoms of depression and Rex talked about the ones that had been bothering him. Jenny gave Rex feedback about changes that she had seen in him, and Rex learned some things about how he had started communicating in a different way. "She told me that I had started to give one-word answers to her questions, when I used to say more." They talked about self-help goals that Rex was working on, and Jenny encouraged her uncle to keep at it. She let him know how proud she was of him for taking responsibility for his recovery.

Initially, Rex met with Jenny every week or so. Sometimes they talked about his recovery over the phone when Jenny could not get away from other responsibilities. After a couple of months, Rex and Jenny both noticed that he had improved a lot. Rex was feeling less hopeless and starting to feel better about himself. Jenny encouraged Rex to start walking at the mall for exercise as a goal, and he met a walking group there that he became friendly with. Rex had established a regular routine for cleaning his house and he felt more organized. Rex and Jenny agreed that they would meet less often, but Jenny made Rex promise that he would call at least once a month to check in about his mood and how he was doing. They both agreed that having Jenny as Rex's coach had helped Rex make it to recovery and had helped them feel closer as a family.

Goal 1: Finding Your Coach

Think of one or two people who could be your coach. Ask to meet with them or talk with them on the phone. Explain that you are experiencing depression and are starting a self-help program that suggests that a coach would be helpful. Ask them if they would be willing to talk with you about your program every week or more often. Suggest a schedule and a start date and time. They must also be willing to talk with you about your goals and give you feedback and suggestions about how you are doing. Tell them a big part of their role as coach will be to encourage you to stick with it. Remind them that they will *not* be your therapist, but a trusted advisor. Be sure to ask them to express any concerns or limitations that they might have in doing this for you (such as that they will be out of town a lot and not be available when you need them). After you have done this, write down the results:

My coach will be:

_____

We are scheduled to meet/phone on the following date and time:

_____

Typical Goals for Recovery

Throughout the remaining chapters of the book, we will suggest goals to help you move forward on specific issues of depression. At this point, though, you are probably thinking of some ideas yourself. Goals do work best if they are designed with you in mind and address specific problems that you have been having since being depressed. In order for you to be able to formulate some goals for yourself, it may help to read about goals that other older adults have used successfully during their recovery from the symptoms of depression. You'll find plenty of examples here.

In all of life's endeavors, there is a beginning, a middle, and an end. In a similar way, the goals that you work on to recover from depression will match the phase you are in. Think of yourself now at the beginning phase there will also be a middle and a final phase. We will concentrate on beginning-phase goals in this chapter and will include more advanced goals in later chapters. Like many people with depression, you probably want to feel better "yesterday!" You may be tempted to start with a goal that is better suited to the final phase. But this is likely to lead to frustration and a desire to quit. It is best to start with simple goals and then work your way up slowly to more complex goals. It is similar to someone starting a diet and exercise program. It would not be realistic for them to expect that they should run a marathon during the first week or lose forty pounds by the second. They need to start building up strength and endurance first before moving to advanced activities. Patience is essential!

Some of the goals will be ongoing things that you will do each day indefinitely. Other goals you will pursue only for a certain time. But it is critical that you set aside a specific time each week to evaluate how you are doing with your goals. This is a good thing to do with your coach.

To be effective, goals must be:

- **Written Down**—When you write down your goals and look at them each day, it really helps you in your commitment to follow through with them. Some people keep them in a notebook so that they can be checked off and updated weekly, while others put them on the refrigerator as a daily reminder.

- **Small**—Break down each desired goal into small steps. You will start with the small steps, one at a time. For example, before you were depressed, reading one chapter of a book would have been easy. With depression, however, it is more realistic for you to have a goal to read three pages of a book in a day. As you improve, you will be able to increase the number of pages. Allow yourself time to improve slowly.

- **Measurable**—How will you know if the goal is working or not, unless you can measure it? You may get discouraged if you only have vague references for your progress such as, "I felt a little bit better about that today." Measuring the outcome of your goals includes being able to do something a certain number of times a week or for a specified time. For instance, you may decide to have as a goal that you will identify one negative thought each day. It may also be something that you can record by writing down or rating it.

- **Achievable**—Many people aspire to complete goals that are simply not realistic. A person who has had a stroke wants to return to driving by the end of the month because he knows driving will help his self-esteem. However, he is still having problems with his balance. It is more valuable to his emotional wellness to work on goals now related to enhancing his mobility rather than to set himself up for failure and disappointment. For example, this person may have as a goal to do the exercises that he did with a physical therapist two times daily to build his strength and balance. He will build confidence in his ability to get around more independently. Working toward this goal will help him eventually get to his larger goal of driving.

Some people get into trouble when they evaluate how they did with their goals. Negative thinking can cause you to be overly critical of yourself. You will learn more about this in chapter 4. Do not expect perfection, especially when you are just starting out. If it is taking you longer than two weeks to complete a certain goal, you may need to look at it closely. Did you expect to do too many complicated steps at one time? You may be expecting too much of yourself based on how you felt before you were depressed or even when you were younger. You will want to either rewrite the goal or drop it. At the same time, you need to ask yourself if you actually did the work for the goal—or did you just think about it one day and get overwhelmed? Look at your results honestly and openly. Talk about this with your coach. Accept the results and move on.

Starting Out

In the beginning phase you realize that you have depression, and you come to the conclusion that you must and can do something about it. Your symptoms are intense, however, and you may have limited energy and motivation. Your goals will be simple and very small. The emphasis will be on taking care of yourself in a more mindful and generous way than you have been. Once you know what your symptoms are, you can gear your goals toward lessening them. These initial goals will serve as steps toward larger goals.

Examples

- Joanna is told by her family doctor that she is depressed. The doctor gives her a list of the symptoms of depression. Joanna is initially troubled by the diagnosis, but as she thinks about it, she knows that something has been very wrong. Joanna wrote her goal this way: *I will read the list of symptoms of depression and check off the ones that seem familiar to me. I will talk about these symptoms with at least one other person (such as my coach) so that I can get their view as well.*

  This is an excellent starting goal, and if you have not already done this after reading chapter 1, do it now!

- Maria feels so depressed that she doesn't eat. She has to push herself to eat anything. She has lost weight and feels tired all the time. She wrote her goal to improve how she takes care of herself this way: *I will eat three nutritious meals each day, even if in small quantities at first; increase my intake of fluids over a week to drink six to eight glasses of water each day; and walk for five minutes at least three times this week. I will record each of these in a notebook to keep track of how I am doing.*

  This goal deals with the following symptoms: depressed mood, poor appetite, poor concentration, and fatigue.

- Julio is terribly negative about everything in his life. Sleep is bad, food tastes terrible, he can't do anything that he wants to do, his arthritis is worse, nobody cares if he lives or dies. His negativity is driving his family crazy, so they avoid talking to him. Julio knows this but can't seem to stop himself—and it makes him feel worse. He wrote his goal this way: *I will have one hour a day for a week when I do not say a single negative thing. I can't just spend the hour alone; I have to be with someone or call someone. Then I'll talk to whomever I was with and get feedback about how I did. Then I'll write down how it felt for me to do this.*

  This goal is useful if you have the following symptoms: feelings of hopelessness, depressed mood, thoughts of death, fatigue, and poor concentration.

- Theresa has become very isolated as she has gotten depressed. Now she avoids talking to anyone. Many of her friends have died and her family is scattered across the country. Before she got depressed, she enjoyed traveling to visit them, but now she feels hopeless and helpless and alone in her apartment. She wrote her goal like this: *I will make one phone call every day to a friend or a family member and talk for at least a few minutes.*

  This goal is useful if you are having: feelings of worthlessness, social withdrawal, or depressed mood.

- George has had much trouble sleeping. He tends to start worrying at bedtime about things that he cannot control. He tosses and turns and feels increasingly nervous and anxious. He wonders where his confidence has gone. He feels like a wreck the next day. George wrote his goal as: *I will practice deep breathing for two to three minutes twice a day to help myself focus and get less tense. I will also practice this at night as I prepare for bed.* (See chapter 7 for details about methods for deep breathing exercises.)

    This goal will help with the following symptoms: sleeplessness, restlessness, feelings of worthlessness, depressed mood, and poor concentration.

- Rosa also has had problems sleeping. For years, she has had a glass or two of wine before bedtime, thinking that this would help. She has now learned that alcohol is contraindicated with depression and it is likely the wine is disrupting her sleep more than it helps. Also, her doctor would like her to try an antidepressant medication that may help with sleep, but he advised her that she should cut out the alcohol first. Here is Rosa's goal: *Each night I will decrease the amount of wine that I am drinking. I'll do this over a few days until I am not drinking any alcohol at all. I will monitor myself for a few days afterward for any signs of discomfort or craving and discuss how I am doing with my doctor.*

    You will benefit from this goal if you have similar problems with the symptoms of sleep disturbance and depressed mood.

- Victor also has problems with sleep but in the opposite direction. He does not want to get up in the morning. His son tries calling him to cajole him into getting up, but Victor does not answer the phone. He forces himself out of bed at 10 A.M. After eating something, he falls asleep in front of the television. He stays in his pajamas most of the day, and talks himself out of showering most days. Victor's goal is: *I will get up each day at 8:30 A.M., shower and shave, get dressed and eat breakfast. I will call my son and talk to him about how I am doing.*

    This goal addresses these symptoms: depressed mood, fatigue, feelings of hopelessness, social withdrawal, and low self-esteem.

- Howard was an accountant, and his friends kidded him about his "mind of steel." He was always in control of every fact and number. But after becoming depressed, Howard has worried that his mind has gone awry. He has trouble remembering the simplest things. He feels embarrassed and worries that his memory will only get worse. Thinking about losing his memory and concentration makes Howard feel more depressed and hopeless. Howard's goal is: *I will carry a pocket notebook and a pen with me. I will write down things that I need to remember, such as the grocery list, an errand that I need to take care of tomorrow, or a letter that I need to write. I will check my notebook twice a day at the same time to keep up with what I need to remember.*

This goal can help improve concentration and lessen depressed mood.

• Normally, Mitzi has so many projects going that others are amazed at what she gets done. Lately, since she became depressed, she feels apathetic and restless. She has stopped working on her ceramics and sewing. She doesn't read and she doesn't write in her journal, which she used to do faithfully every day. She feels terrible about this but when she has tried to sit down with one of her projects, she gets frustrated easily and starts to think about how helpless she is. Mitzi's goal is: *I will sit down two days this week for fifteen minutes with my sewing project. I will work for only fifteen minutes. I will tell myself that I am helping myself get better. I will not judge my work harshly or be concerned if I do not particularly enjoy it. When the fifteen minutes is up I will stop.*

This goal is effective and can help you with the symptoms of loss of pleasure, depressed mood, restlessness, poor concentration, and feelings of worthlessness. A part of getting back to doing things that have been pleasurable to you in the past is to just do them, without expectations that you will enjoy it. That will come later as your mood gets better. You will make gains in self-esteem by doing something rather than nothing.

• Since Tom has become depressed, he has become very disorganized. Though he has always prided himself on his ability to take care of his personal business, he has felt too hopeless and tired to even open his mail. About the most he can do is bring the mail in and pile it on top of the other unopened mail on his table. Just looking at this pile makes him feel worthless and ashamed. It is overwhelming. Tom's goal is: *For ten minutes every day over the next week, I will sit at the table and sort my mail. I will get rid of the junk mail and put the bills in a separate pile. I will talk to my coach about how I am doing with this and how I feel when I am done.*

This goal will help you decrease the symptoms of depressed mood, feelings of hopelessness, feelings of low self-esteem, and poor concentration.

Goals and Motivation

You will notice that most of your goals will require that you do some thinking and take some action. People with depression are often puzzled by how they will be able to do more when they feel so tired and unmotivated. The key to overcoming fatigue and lack of motivation is to start small but push yourself to do something. It will be very slow going, but you will notice that something is better than nothing. A positive response will not be instantaneous, but rather a building process. Your thoughts may be fuzzy at first, but with even slight increases in activity and putting your mind to work, you will notice over time that it is easier to get your thoughts organized. Now we will move on to more of your own goals.

Goal 2: Writing Your Own Goals

Remember the two symptoms that you identified earlier as being the worst for you? Your first goals should address those symptoms. Now that you have some ideas about goals that other people have worked on, write down two ideas that you have for goals that you would like to start with:

1. _____

_____

_____

_____

Symptoms addressed: _____

2. _____

_____

_____

_____

Symptoms addressed: _____

Goal 3: Get Organized!

Your work on your goals will flow better if you have prepared your "workspace" in advance. Do you have a notebook or perhaps a computer to use to write down your goals? Do you have a calendar that you can use to organize your week? Do you do better with projects if you can see them posted in a prominent place? Do have a place in your home that will be comfortable and conducive for you to sit down each day and write and think? If your desk is a mess, it will probably be a hindrance rather than a help to work there. When you are depressed, such things as a lack of writing paper or a burnt-out light bulb can easily hold you back by becoming powerful excuses. Write down any tasks that need to be done to improve your workspace or items that you need to have on hand to work on your goals. Include when and how you will take care of these items:

_____

_____

_____

_____

_____

Goal 4: Make the Commitment

One way to keep yourself motivated and working on your goals is to actively make a decision to do them. This will take you from just thinking about them, or "this sounds like a good idea that I might do later," to "I am going to do this and I am starting now."

A written agreement will help. Use the format provided or create one of your own.

I am making a commitment to myself to take active steps to help myself recover from depression. I will work on self-help goals. I will do the best that I can do. I will work on at least one new goal each week and talk about my progress with my coach.

Signature _____

Date _____

Terrific! You are now ready to learn more about helping yourself along the way. Making a commitment and working on goals is one of many healthy lifestyle changes that you can make on your way to recovery from depression. Setting goals can be a major tool to help you keep your momentum and be an active participant in your own life.

Chapter 3

Get Up and Go!
Why Social Connections Are So Important

Your ability to make and keep social connections will help you maintain good mental and physical health. Researchers have found that people who have social support live longer, healthier, and happier lives. Moreover, social support can diminish the impact of some the health-related effects of aging.

Bob's Story

"All my friends have died. I don't want to bother my children—they have busy lives of their own. If I could I would go back to work again. That's when I was happiest. My life was my work. I was respected and people counted on me. Now there is really nothing to look forward to," says Bob.

Bob is eighty years old and retired from the railroad where he worked for over thirty years. Like many other older adults, he was pressured to retire at sixty-five. He has been retired for fifteen years and lost his wife two years ago. He lives in a middle-class neighborhood in the same house he and his wife shared for over thirty years. Bob depended on his wife not only for companionship but also for many of the household chores. Bob and his wife used to know almost everyone in the neighborhood where they lived and could count on a friendly "hello" from someone during the day. Now, most of the neighborhood has changed as older people have either passed away or moved away. Younger families have moved into the neighborhood and hardly anyone talks to each other anymore. The neighborhood where he has lived most of his adult life looks like a strange place to him now. The confidence Bob once had seems to have disappeared, and his life now feels empty and lonesome. A gregarious and kind man, Bob was at a loss to explain his feelings.

Eventually his doctor told Bob that he had symptoms of depression. Bob called his local area agency on aging and asked if there were any counseling groups for older adults. He was able to find a group run by a nurse at an outpatient senior health clinic. With the urging of his children, Bob found the courage to join the group. He began to talk about his fear of meeting other people without his wife by his side. The group setting itself was an example of how difficult it was for him to interact with other people. Bob was uncomfortable being with these unfamiliar people and talking about his feelings.

Bob had previously dismissed going to the senior center, because "there are only old people there." During group therapy he was challenged to take some steps that might be uncomfortable for him. The group encouraged Bob to meet other people and begin to engage in activities he had never before considered. One of the first steps he agreed to do was to go to a senior center and talk to one person there. This was not nearly as hard to do as he thought it would be, and he was surprised to find other widowed men there. His next step was to try one activity at the center. Bob decided to take a computer class and learn how to use the Internet. After a couple of months, he began to feel a little like himself again. He began a slow process of gaining back his confidence by taking these small, supported steps.

Social Involvement as You Age

Picture a young person you know, say in her twenties, who isolated herself in her room day after day, refusing to go out and meet people. You would be alarmed and concerned about this young person's mental state. Why should it be any different for an older adult?

Social support, relationships, and community are just as important now as they were when you were younger—if not more so. However, there may be some challenges to finding and maintaining social connections as you get older. Bob's experience is common to many older adults. Career and family have most likely occupied your life in significant ways. Your collective social experience is in large part a product of the many roles you have assumed throughout your adult life. Once those roles are no longer relevant or prevalent, your social experience may change.

You may feel that no one can replace dear and close friends from the past and that you don't want new friends. For some people, loyal feelings for past friends who have died or moved away hold them back from reaching out to new people and relationships. However, it's important to understand and accept that you will not be replacing the friends you once had. New friendships may not have the same degree of closeness, but they can still enrich your life in numerous ways. Each relationship is different, but they're all valuable.

Don't let expectations keep you from enjoying the company of the many new people you will meet. All of your friends of the past would want it that way. And who knows, perhaps you will be pleasantly surprised at the positive and stimulating relationships you develop as you age.

You've probably heard the expression that the only constant is change. In many respects this is never more true than when you age. We have talked about the challenges of aging in a culture that is just beginning to appreciate and nurture the collective wisdom, experience, and expertise of older adults. The changing roadmap of aging is full of unexpected curves and detours, and depression makes the journey that much more difficult.

As you read this chapter and begin to open yourself up to new experiences, keep in mind how vital a sense of community is to your well-being. Regardless of size, location, or definition, community is vital for our survival and happiness, and arguably never more relevant than as we get older. It takes work to find community, and then it requires a lifelong commitment to keeping your community alive and vibrant. Each of your communities gives you resources: some that you will use now, and others you may need later.

You must value yourself and maintain the resolve to create your own communities where you find them lacking. "Productivity" is a term that has been defined in our society to a large extent as it relates to work or family. Productivity through aging is beginning to have a myriad of meanings that reflect the diversity and value of the collective experience of hundreds of thousands of older adults. As demographics change, so do our communities. If you can embrace these changes as opportunities, you will have a good chance of enriching your life and the lives of others in ways you never thought possible.

You may be interested in meeting and interacting with your peers, but have little idea how to go about it. You *can* assume new roles, experience new activities, and challenge even your own deep-seated assumptions about improving and changing your social experience. This can occur whether you are homebound or independent and active. Dramatic and significant change can occur at any age!

The First Step: Know Your Social Style

Having depression can make it even more difficult to find the energy and motivation to reach out to peers and family at a time when their support is crucial. You may feel tired and irritable and simply not care whether you see anyone or not. You probably prefer not to be socially active at this time. Recall in chapter 1 the discussion about how difficult it is to reveal feelings of depression. When you are depressed, it can affect those close to you. Friends, family, and associates may detect some difference in your general demeanor and outlook. Perhaps a family member or friend remarks on your "orneriness" or bad temper. They don't understand why you don't "get out of the house and do something!" Family and friends may notice changes, but may misinterpret what those changes mean and become confused, distressed, or feel responsible for your lack of social involvement. Relationships can become strained.

In talking about social interactions, depression, and communication, it is important to know what your "social style" is. There is a difference between feeling lonely and being a loner. Some people are comfortable and happy spending more time alone. Knowing your social personality style will help you to evaluate how depression is affecting your ability to interact and communicate with others. Identifying your style will also help you to honestly evaluate what your social expectations are. For example, if you are the shy and retiring type, you may need to step out of your comfort zone and try on a more assertive style. If you are typically the life of the party, you may benefit from taking more time to yourself or spending more quiet time with people one on one.

Exercise: How You Relate to Other People

Take a moment to identify your personality style. Write down your impressions of how you have typically related to people in your adult life.

_____

_____

_____

_____

_____

You are not a slave to your style of relating to other people. But it *is* easy to get trapped into thinking that you have only one way in which to socially interact with others. When you are depressed, it may be necessary to break the mold a bit and take some chances with people. You may not even remember what you were like socially, or you may feel that you have lost the ability to relate to people.

You may not want to let other people know that you are having problems with depression, or, on the other hand, you may feel more comfortable confiding in certain people you trust. The choice is entirely up to you. Here are some tips to help facilitate communication when you are depressed.

- **Recognize that people are generally more understanding and approachable than we expect them to be.** If you have a fear of rejection or judgment by others, try to understand that people generally reject or judge others because of something they don't understand or feel comfortable with. If by chance you encounter someone who doesn't understand what you are going through, or isn't interested in getting to know you, move on and try not to worry about someone you can't change.

- **Practice talking with one of your coaches.** You might want to try out some of the exercises in this chapter with him or her; or perhaps you will want to see how it feels to role-play a session where you initiate conversation with someone new. It can be very helpful to practice talking with someone who you feel is impartial and will give you feedback on how you do.

- **Don't expect to feel like being social before you start taking some action steps.** You may wait a long, long time to improve if you expect to "feel good" before making any decisions about getting better. You will need to start acting socially now, regardless of how difficult it may be at first. Your feelings will start to gradually change as you take action steps to improve your social life.

Social Interactions Can Keep You Healthy and Happy

Let's look at some of the reasons social support is so important, whether you are nineteen or 109, and whether you are depressed or not.

- **Social interactions are stimulating to the brain.** Learning develops new connections in the brain that can act as a buffer against diseases like Alzheimer's. An example of this can be something as simple as having regular conversations with others, participating in group discussions, attending lectures, or taking classes. Of course social interaction is not a necessary component of learning, but social support and interaction provide the health-related benefits of increased longevity, protection from the "damaging health effects of stressful life situations," and improved quality of life (Rowe and Kahn 1998, p. 157). Mental stimulation provides psychological benefits and may even change brain anatomy in ways that limit age-related declines in mental functioning.

- **Interacting with others gives you the opportunity to share and exchange ideas, which in turn increases self-esteem and builds self-confidence.** Many times in your life, you have experienced the joy and satisfaction of giving someone advice or comfort. Think about a time when you shared an opinion about something you believe in and how that made you feel. You have a lifetime of experiences, talents, and skills to share. Social exchanges and interactions are the building blocks of self-esteem. Learning to comfortably interact with others is a lifelong skill that requires continual practice and honing. The longer you remain isolated, the more difficult it becomes to engage with people.

- **Social isolation leads to poor coping skills, which makes it more difficult to deal effectively with stress.** The ability to manage stress has been identified as an important factor in longevity and health. People who are able to manage their stress effectively live longer, happier lives. If you isolate yourself, you don't have the benefit of feedback or help from others. The mind becomes dulled by lack of stimulating activities. Your judgment about your ability to handle stress can become distorted. Being around others gives you a more balanced view of the world by providing some perspective. Learning to handle stress effectively keeps you healthy and happy at any age.

Let's look at some examples of social interaction and support.

- **Telephone conversations with relatives, neighbors, friends, or clergy.** Regular phone conversations are a great way to stay in touch with people and enjoy the comfort of your home. If you aren't able to get out of your house very often, talking on the phone is especially valuable.

- **Visiting with relatives, friends, neighbors, or clergy.** Call and ask someone if you can drop by for a short visit. They will probably be grateful for the company.

- **Involvement in organizations or religious groups.** Check your newspaper, the Internet, or Aging Services, or ask a friend if they know of organizations that you may enjoy. Volunteer opportunities such as senior companion programs, foster grandparent programs, senior employment, church groups, and many others are plentiful for seniors. You may even decide you are interested in going back to work part-time.

- **Going to the senior center or to other older adult group activities.** We will mention senior centers several times in this chapter because they are generally wonderful places to meet people and learn new activities. There are plenty of other adult groups to investigate, from hiking and gardening groups to discussion and reading groups.

- **Spending time on the Internet chatting with other seniors.** Especially if you are alone, being on the Internet can give you a sense of a larger community of like-minded people. You can exchange ideas, have conversations, and learn new information about everything from senior resources to medical information.

You Can Rise to the Challenge

Admittedly, there are many challenges to finding and maintaining social relationships as you age. Being depressed may make these challenges seem insurmountable, but here are some potential challenges and possible solutions to each:

"But I'm Not Driving Anymore!"

- Contact your local area agency on aging and find out what transportation is available through your city, county, or state.

- If you have found a place you would like to go, whether it is a senior center, a class, or the library, talk to someone at the facility and inquire about carpooling with another participant.

- Ask a family member or friend to provide limited transportation for you on a scheduled basis.

- Take a bus, the train, or other public transportation. Call your local transit authority for a map of routes. Ask about possible training to learn how to use the system.

- Pay for a taxi.

"I Don't Know Where My Opportunities Are."

- First, find out what does exist in your area by calling your local Area Agency on Aging. Don't assume that you already know what is available.

- Create your own group by calling friends and getting their suggestions on activities you can do together at someone's home or in a public space such as the library or a church. These activities may be playing cards, learning new recipes, woodworking, a book club, or discussion groups with predetermined topics. The possibilities are limitless.

- If you don't have a computer, consider purchasing a Web TV that will give you access to the World Wide Web and allow you to communicate with other seniors around the world by e-mail. A Web TV setup, which costs a fraction of the cost of a computer, is a device that can be connected to any television set. It consists of a keyboard and an apparatus about the size of a VCR and is available at most major department and electronic stores. It requires a monthly fee through your phone service to have access to the Internet. One of the major advantages of being connected to the Internet and using e-mail is that you can be virtually homebound and not be isolated. It can't take the place of face-to-face contact, but it can be a rewarding and invigorating hobby. Parents e-mail their children, grandparents e-mail their grandkids, and people communicate with one another from around the world.

- If the Internet is something you are afraid to tackle, find someone to help you set up a computer or Web TV and show you how to use it. Dive in and learn from trial and error. There are literally hundreds of Web sites for seniors. In the Resources section, we've listed just a few of them. Look in your local paper or call your senior center or college/university to see where you might be able to take a class on how to use the Internet.

- Explore the availability of support groups for Hispanics/Latinos, African-Americans, Asians, gays and lesbians, or any other cultural, religious, or ethnic group.

"I Don't Know What My Role in Life Is Now."

- Admittedly, this may be a more complicated problem to address because it involves how you feel about yourself and the importance that we as a society place on being "productive." However, opportunities abound for you to find new and interesting ways to express yourself and find success. We will talk more about these opportunities shortly. It is entirely possible, and advisable, for you to be open to new ways of feeling good about yourself. Success and productivity can be measured and experienced in many different ways.

"I Don't Want to Hang Around Old People."

• If we had a dollar for every time we have heard an older person say, "I don't want to go to a senior center. There are old people there!," we would be rich. Confront your own unrealistic and biased views about aging and how they influence what you do and don't do. Some questions to ask: Does seeing older, frailer people bring up your own fears about aging? Do you think that you won't find older adults similar to yourself at senior centers or other settings that cater to seniors? Do you have concerns that a senior center's programming will be childish? If these issues bother you, make inquiries about the kinds of activities you are interested in and ask about the participants at the center. Talk to the programming manager about finding an instructor for a particular class. Consider teaching a class yourself! Don't make assumptions about a setting or an experience until you have given it a chance. One visit will not be enough to accurately evaluate the experience. If you see people older and frailer than yourself, notice your reaction and try to examine your feelings. Talk with your coach about how realistic your concerns are. Once you have visited a senior center, revisit your initial thoughts and assess their accuracy. Some of them may be legitimate, so you will need to evaluate whether this particular senior center will meet your needs. If it doesn't, at least you have given it a fair chance. Nothing ventured, nothing gained.

"What Possible Value Could I Be to My Community?"

• Whether you realize it or not, you *are* a resource to your community. Think about your hobbies, skills, and experience. What are some of the characteristics of your personality that are helpful and supportive? What do you have to give other people? Be bold and confident in your assessment of what you have to offer, regardless of how small it may seem.

Where to Go and What to Do

Here are some ideas on how to meet other people, both young and old.

Retirement Communities/Assisted Living

Many older adults who live in retirement communities don't take advantage of the activities offered there. We've heard many older adults say, "There's nothing going on at night," or " I don't like the activities that they have going on here." Most places have a calendar of events and activities. If you are dissatisfied with the types or times of activities listed, talk with your housing or activities director. Make some suggestions. Get other residents to support you. One of the advantages to living in an assisted living facility or retirement home is the social environment. Seek out those people who have similar interests. Keep in mind that it is often easier to meet people while engaged in an activity. In some communities, people are getting together and buying property or housing and making their own communities. This is referred to as cooperative housing.

Senior Centers

Senior centers vary from state to state, and even within communities, but in general they are excellent places to meet other older adults. We have heard numerous older adults make the comment, "This place has been a godsend to me." Senior centers offer a variety of recreational and educational activities, including computer classes, dance, exercise, ceramics, group discussions, trips, and much more. You might feel nervous before your first visit. If so, it may be helpful for you to call ahead and make certain that someone will be available to show you around. Sign up for classes right away so you can get to know other participants and avoid procrastination. Senior centers across the country are attempting to rise to the challenge of meeting the needs of two and sometimes three generations of older adults.

Groups

Most metropolitan areas have a variety of self-help and support groups. These may include groups for grief and loss, depression, and self-esteem. There is also support for a variety of ethnic groups from Asians and Bosnians to Hispanics/Latinos and African-Americans. Gays and lesbians have support groups, although communities will differ in the availability of support for older gays and lesbians. Religious organizations have a variety of support systems. There are Jewish, Catholic, Quaker, Unitarian, Tibetan, and other Protestant and Christian groups that often provide support whether you are a member of that particular church or not. Call your local Area Agency on Aging or information and referral service (which in some communities provides information to consumers on a variety of social service agencies) to find out about groups in your area. You may need to make multiple calls to find what you are looking for, so don't get discouraged.

Aging Services

Your local Area Agency on Aging has a wealth of information on programs, services, employment, and opportunities for seniors. Their number is in the blue pages of the phone book. In chapter 3 we will talk in more detail about Aging Services across the country.

Elderhostel

Elderhostel is a program for seniors offering educational and recreational opportunities worldwide. Typically these are weeklong learning adventures for older adults from around the world. Some Elderhostels place more of an emphasis on activity, whereas others are more geared toward learning. It is not unusual for many Elderhostel attendees at any given location to be widowed or be there alone by choice. So if you are concerned about being with a group of strangers, don't be. You will be in good company! See the Resources section in the back of this book for information on how to contact Elderhostel.

The World Wide Web

If you don't have a computer or Web TV and can afford one, get it. If not, check your local senior center or library. They often have computers available for public use and offer instruction as well. The advantages of learning how to use the Internet are numerous. They include being able to access news twenty-four hours a day, find information specifically for seniors on hundreds of Web sites, send e-mail and "chat" with others on line, and find medical and any other information in a matter of minutes.

Exercise: What Activities Do You Do Now?

Let's start where you are now so you will have a better idea of where you need to go and what you need to do to become more socially involved.

_____

_____

_____

_____

_____

Evaluate these activities in terms of how much they involve other people. You can spend too much of your time involved in activities that are solitary. Solitary activities are important to have, but not at the expense of spending some of your time with other people.

Exercise: Other Activities You Have an Interest in Trying

Now, take a moment and identify some other areas that you haven't tried that interest you. We will repeat this activity later in the chapter, but for now, view this exercise as a way to expose your fears. Be aware of "yes, but" statements that sabotage your efforts. For every excuse you come up with not to try a new activity, problem-solve that excuse. Write down possible solutions to barriers or challenges. Put your mind to it and view social opportunities as necessities that will enable you to benefit in all the ways we have mentioned. You will be amazed at the difference it will make in the quality of your life.

_____

_____

_____

_____

Let's Get Started

Being depressed, you may feel like being left alone—or you may feel like you are being left out. As part of your recovery, you will need to learn how to overcome feelings of loneliness, isolation, and apathy. Do you feel lonely? What time of day or day of the week do you feel your worst? Use this checklist to learn more about how you feel.

When do you feel most isolated or lonely?

☐ during the day

☐ at night

☐ on the weekends

☐ during holidays

☐ when I am with family or friends

Many people say they feel very alone and isolated even when they are with other people. By looking at when you feel your worst, you will be able to tailor your social engagement to fit those tough times.

The best way to change your feelings is to change your behavior. However, identifying the feelings and thoughts that guide your behavior will help you recognize the powerful influence they have over you.

Patrick's Story

Patrick is an eighty-two-year-old man who had a long and successful career as a university professor. He has been retired for just five years, having worked up until the age of seventy-seven. He lives in a comfortable suburb of a major city and has a loving wife, two children, and three grandchildren. Shortly after his retirement, Patrick became increasingly depressed. He complained of feelings of frustration, loneliness, and boredom. He experienced trouble sleeping at night and had no appetite during the day.

Patrick's wife, Connie, had been socially active for years. She belonged to a card club, went swimming two days a week with friends, and talked with other friends over the phone regularly. Connie couldn't fathom how an educated man like Patrick could refuse to join a club or call some of his university friends. She became irritated with his expressions of boredom and his bad attitude. Connie had given up a career so she could stay home and raise a family while her husband worked. She resented Patrick's inability to make a life for himself now that he was retired.

Finally, with a considerable amount of coaxing, Patrick began to see a therapist. In therapy Patrick talked about how his work was his life—that his self-worth was based entirely on his work achievements and accomplishments. He said he had no idea how to make friends or learn new activities, and even if he did, they couldn't give him the excitement and respect that he came to expect as a professor.

With time, Patrick was able to consider trying something completely different in an effort to cope with the miserable feelings he was having. His therapist talked him into going to the local senior center. He decided to try a sculpting class—something he had never even thought about before. Much to his surprise, he not only enjoyed the sculpting, but also discovered that he was good at it. In the course of taking the class he met other people at the senior center and experienced his next surprise: He met people he liked and could talk to.

Gradually Patrick's self-confidence came back in a way he never expected it would. His depression began to lift and his relationship with his wife improved. He gained some understanding about how much he had neglected other parts of his life when he was working.

What Do You Expect?

Change occurs on many different levels. Even though you think you know yourself, you may be surprised to find how capable you are of making some significant, lasting improvements in your life. Everyone has expectations about relationships, but acknowledging that some changes may be necessary will help you to move forward. Expecting that social relationships will remain the same as they used to be is unrealistic. Many of the relationships you have formed in the past may have come naturally from your involvement in work, community, or family. These social institutions provide ready-made social arenas that make it easier to form friendships. Perhaps you participated in work parties, family get-togethers, or church activities. These arenas may still be available to you, but on a more limited basis. Or perhaps you relied upon a spouse or partner who is no longer with you to make your social connections. You could have physical or geographical constraints. Regardless of what may have changed, it may be necessary for you to think in new ways about forming and appreciating relationships.

Exercise: What Do You Want in a Relationship?

Are honesty or trust important? How about stimulating conversation, or respect for your privacy? You may find that what was once important in a relationship has changed through the years. As you complete this exercise, also keep in mind that there are different types of relationships that fulfill different needs. You may enjoy casual relationships with people whom you see at the senior center, club, or church group. Other relationships may be based on a sharing of important ideas and experiences.

List the five most important qualities of a relationship for you.

1. _____

2. _____

3. _____

4. _____

5. _____

Take a moment to reflect on what you have written. Can you identify core values or what is most important to you? Have your needs changed? Are you unsure about what you want and need in a relationship right now? Although you may not have the answers to these questions, thinking about them will help you to be more open and aware of what relationships mean to you.

Exercise: The Four Things You Fear Most

Now, let's explore your fears about forming new relationships. Perhaps you fear rejection, or don't feel that you have the skills necessary to form new friendships. You may not have the confidence you once did to initiate contact and carry on a conversation. Perhaps past difficulties in forming relationships have become amplified as you have gotten older. Social institutions may have provided a context in which to talk about things. Now you may feel at a loss as to what to talk about with other people.

1. _____

_____

2. _____

_____

3. _____

_____

4. _____

_____

Take a close look at your attitudes. How realistic are they? Do you suspect that other people have the same concerns about relationships? Granted, your emotional condition may color your perspective on these issues. Discuss these feelings with your coach. One of your concerns may be that a relationship will not give you what you need. Recognize that when you focus on what is not received, you miss out on much of what is given. This may seem like compromising your values, but sometimes lowering your expectations can open new and unanticipated vistas. Your fears and expectations are powerful emotions that keep you from moving forward. In Patrick's story we see an example of how his social expectations and experience revolved around his work. Acknowledge your fears, but commit to moving past them. Believe that you have the power and the obligation to change your feelings and your behavior. Practicing being social will help you to build your self-confidence.

Negative Thoughts Slow You Down

Negative thinking is discussed in more detail in chapter 4, but you'll want to remember starting now that these self-destructive thoughts can sabotage your efforts. Challenging your negative thoughts will help you to move forward. See if any of these thoughts sound familiar:

"I'm too old to make new friends."

"I have nothing to offer someone else my age."

"I couldn't possibly learn to do that."

"There are too many problems for me to do that."

"What difference will it make?"

You most likely have additional negative thoughts that keep you from making social connections. Assume that most of them are either untrue or have solutions to them. You have control over these thoughts. For every negative thought you have, replace it with a positive one. Here are some possible responses to the negative thoughts listed above.

"I'm too old to make new friends."

"I am never too old to make new friends."

"I have nothing to offer someone else my age."

"I have a lifetime of experience and many talents to share with others."

"I couldn't possibly learn to do that."

"I can learn anything I put my mind to."

"There are too many problems for me to do that."

"I can solve my problems one step at a time."

"What difference will it make?"

"I have faith that whatever I try will bring me something good."

Exercise: Do Away with Negative Thinking!

List your negative thoughts about socialializing below. Follow each thought with a positive statement.

Negative Thought: _____

Positive Thought: _____

Negative Thought: _____

Positive Thought: _____

Negative Thought: _____

Positive Thought: _____

Experience and Explore

It can be helpful to investigate your opportunities first without actually taking any action just yet. Take some time to think about what really does interest you. Although you may not feel up to engaging in social activity, encourage yourself to explore the many opportunities available to you. Now it's time to try another goal.

Goal 5: Choose Activities You Would Love to Do

First, identify six activities you have an interest in. List these interests without regard to your ability to do them. Allow your imagination to run wild and think of all the activities you have wanted to try but never have. Or, select activities that you may have dropped, or would like to get better at. Next, go to the phone book, Area Agency on Aging, newspaper, or Internet to find out where you can participate in these activities. Go down your list, making a note of where you might be able to participate in each activity, the contact person, and the phone number.

1. _____

Location and Phone Number:_____

2. _____

Location and Phone Number:_____

3. _____

Location and Phone Number:_____

4. _____

Location and Phone Number:_____

5. _____

Location and Phone Number: _____

6. _____

Location and Phone Number: _____

Ready, Set, Engage!

Now it is time to try something new. This can be a very frightening proposition. But remember: Keep your unrealistic expectations out of the equation! Look at the experience as an experiment in which success is solely measured by virtue of having tried something different.

Goal 6: Ready, Select, Go!

Now, select two of the above activities and call to inquire about the time and location, cost, skill level, and length of commitment. If you aren't satisfied with these two activities, choose two more to investigate. *Be aware of "yes but" statements that may be inhibiting you.*

1. _____

2. _____

Now choose one of the activities you have listed above. Make arrangements to participate in that activity, whether it means signing up for a class or going to the senior center. If for some reason one of the activities doesn't work out, choose the other one. Bookmark this page so that you can come back to it once you have completed the activity. It may take days or weeks to complete this goal—it will be an ongoing endeavor.

Activity: _____

Outcome: _____

_____

_____

Activity: _____

Outcome: _____

_____

_____

If things do not go well with an activity, just chalk it up to bad luck or circumstances beyond your control. An experience that doesn't go as planned is just that: an experience that didn't go as planned. Take a step back, look at the positive things that did happen, and make a note of them. Keep trying new things. Always assume that there is something positive about each experience you have. If necessary, list a few positive things about a disappointing experience.

Practice makes perfect. Once is not enough. It can take time, especially when you are depressed, to try new activities and feel comfortable doing them. Don't be hard on yourself; talk to your coach about how you are doing.

Goal 7: Be Your Own Social Secretary

Remember that we discussed the importance of changing your behavior as a way of changing the way you feel. You may feel uncertain of yourself around other people or simply not be interested in social engagement. This goal will ask you to behave in ways that may not match the way you currently feel. *Just do it! You will feel better later.*

Identify two people you have not talked to in a while; or, if you are up to it, pick someone you have never spoken to before. You may want to pick someone who is lonely and needs someone to talk to. Either call them on the phone, arrange to see them in person, or simply strike up a conversation. Possible people you might want to consider talking to are: neighbors, church members, family, a stranger at the senior center, or friends you haven't seen in a while.

Practice talking and listening to this individual. Listening is a skill that we can all improve upon. One of the best ways to engage another person is to ask them about themselves. This takes the pressure off of you and will help you to practice really listening to what the other person has to say. The skill of listening helps to improve concentration and focus; it facilitates empathy; and it will attract people to you. It has been said that we miss most of what someone says to us. Listening is a lifelong skill that can be honed and used at any age and in any endeavor. Here are some of the basics of listening:

Quiet your mind. You may notice that while someone is talking, you are already thinking about what you are going to say next, or you may be thinking about something totally unrelated to what is being said. Concentrate on just listening, without thinking about how you are going to respond or what you are planning to have for dinner!

Show that you are interested. If you are face to face with the person, maintain good eye contact and keep an open, relaxed posture. If you are on the phone, give verbal indications that you are being attentive by asking questions and making comments about the topic being discussed. In person or over the phone, refrain from interrupting.

Prompt and clarify. To keep the conversation going, make comments like: "Really? Are you sure? Tell me more, that's very interesting."

Goal 8: How Did I Do and What Did I Learn?

In the space below, write down the names of two people you've chosen to speak with this week. After you've gone ahead and had a conversation with them, use the space under "Outcome of conversation" to write down how the attempt went. Examine how well you did with the listening skills. Did you feel awkward or uncomfortable? Did your depression come up in the conversation? Were you unsure of what to say about how you are doing?

If it seems appropriate, arrange to meet with one of these people for a future activity.

1. Name of person: _____

Outcome of conversation: _____

_____

_____

2. Name of person: _____

Outcome of conversation: _____

_____

_____

Repeat this goal once a week until you gain some confidence in your interactions. Practice your listening skills. Remember that you build your listening skills through repeated practice.

Now, take this goal one step further by leaving the house to go to a senior center, party, family get-together, or other activity where there are several people. Pick a person you don't know, or someone you don't usually talk to. Initiate a conversation and practice your listening skills.

Place: _____

Person: _____

Outcome of conversation: _____

_____

_____

_____

Learning (or relearning) how to socially interact will provide you with life-long support and stimulation. You will feel connected to a larger, interactive world of your peers and others. Experiencing new activities sets you on a path to discovering things about yourself you may never have known before. As an older adult with depression, it is up to you to pave this road to recovery, and in the process you will gain so much more from life. As Dale Carnegie said, "You can make more friends in two months by becoming interested in other people than you can in two years trying to get other people interested in you."

Chapter 4

How to Master Your Thoughts and Build Your Self-Esteem

Like many people with depression, you may be plagued by unhappy and hopeless thoughts. Negative thoughts can have a destructive impact on your outlook and behavior. By deciding to challenge these thoughts, you can make a change in your attitude and your life.

Ted's Story

Ted, a seventy-eight-year-old former accountant, lost his wife ten years ago to cancer. He retired two years later. He relates how these events started a stressful period in his life that led to depression:

"I had not wanted to retire at that time and felt at the end that I was being forced into it. I felt that my colleagues at work had abandoned me, and I felt betrayed. I had never experienced anything like it, so my retirement, which I had once looked forward to, didn't get off to such a great start. I didn't realize, I guess because I was suddenly spending so much time alone, how much my attitude had changed. I don't think that it happened overnight. I would spend hours thinking about everything that had happened at work, and after a while, I couldn't think about anything else. I began to feel worse and worse about myself. I would think, 'If only I had been smarter or younger, they would not have pushed me to get out of there.' My children would invite me out to dinner but I believed I would just bring them down, so I'd make excuses not to go. I started to doubt how well I was managing my bills and just stopped taking care of them. They were piling up in a corner and it just paralyzed me to look at them. I couldn't believe it. This from me who always paid on time, on the dot, never late. I felt more and more ashamed. I finally talked to my doctor about how I was feeling and he sent me to a therapist. It was such a relief to talk to someone about all the thoughts I was having.

"As I started to get better, I began to see how the depression had changed how I was looking at the world and at myself. I had always been an upbeat kind of fellow, and I wanted to get back to that, to my old self. I remember one day that I got tired of thinking about all of these things and just sort of started talking back to myself, and that really helped."

Taking Charge of Your Thoughts

In this chapter, we will look at the connection between your thinking and your self-esteem. In addition, we will look at how you can take action to change your thoughts so you feel better about yourself. When you are depressed, it may take more than one approach to chip away at negative thoughts. There are exercises that you can do along the way that will help you learn more about how these thoughts may be controlling your life. Take your time to do each one, even if you write something very brief. Then, complete the goals of this chapter when you are not reading the book. The goals will present strategies that have helped other older adults to release themselves from negative thoughts and rebuild their self-esteem. Working on them will give you the opportunity to start practicing healthier ways of dealing with these thoughts every day.

For some people with depression, it is unclear which started first—the change in their mood or the negative thoughts. Either way, the negativity seems to take on a life of its own. It may be hard for you to remember a time when you did not have so many negative thoughts. Or, you notice that there has been a more recent change in your usual attitude about life and yourself. This change in thinking may be described as being "down about everything." To make matters worse, a sense of guilt develops because of your inability to overcome intense and distressing negative thoughts. Perhaps you wonder why you cannot simply tell yourself to get over it. But "getting over it" is not as easy as it sounds.

It is essential to remember that you are having thoughts that have a powerful effect on your emotional state. This reduces your ability to be objective about these thoughts and actually encourages you to be unfair to yourself. You become more pessimistic and sound more cynical and even angry. You might notice a change in your tone of voice. Perhaps you are speaking more quietly or finding it harder to look other people in the face. You may be communicating your doubts about yourself and your life in more ways than you realize.

Exercise: Get to Know Your Attitude

How would you describe your overall outlook on life? Write down any thoughts about what you consider to be your usual attitude about life:

_____

_____

_____

Now write down any changes in your attitude that you have noticed since you started feeling depressed:

_____

_____

_____

_____

Be Your Own Best Friend

Think about a good friend of yours. Imagine that friend came to you and said, "You know, I'm just not the person I used to be. I really think that I am worthless. My life is terrible. I probably was never very good at those things that I thought I was good at, and my family probably would agree." Most likely, you would be amazed at your friend's sudden loss of connection to the truth. You would realize that he or she is a valuable, contributing member of society, with many talents and well loved. You might respond by refuting your friend's misconceptions. You would remind him or her of specific reasons that these thoughts are untrue, such as, "You have been helpful to others and even now your family relies on your good advice and counsel. You are still the best bridge player in our group, and you could also teach a lot of younger folks about the history of this state. You are a good person with a great sense of humor that everyone appreciates." In other words, you would present the realistic evidence to disprove the negative thoughts.

With the same direct and reasonable attention, you must examine your own thinking. But even though you would immediately recognize them in a good friend, it is often quite challenging to identify your own negative, distorted thoughts. Negative thoughts are sometimes referred to as negative "self-talk," because it is like an ongoing conversation that you are having with yourself. You may have become so accustomed to these thoughts being a part of your mental landscape that you hardly notice them. They are there so much of the time that you no longer think about questioning them. So, it may be a bit like catching butterflies at first. But with practice, you will spot them with more certainty.

Unsure of what your negative thoughts may sound like? Here are some examples:

- "I can never think of the right thing to say."

- "I will never get this house cleaned up."

- "My family would be better off if I were dead."

- "I'm sure there is nothing that would interest me at the senior center."

- "If my son really loved me, he would call more often."

- "If people really knew me, they wouldn't like me."

When your mind is filled with negative thoughts, it becomes almost impossible to consider more positive ones. Your focus becomes narrower and narrower and less open to new possibilities. The thoughts cause a number of emotional responses. You don't feel good when you are having negative thoughts, because the thoughts cause a chain reaction that results in a bad feeling. Try to become aware of your feelings, such as uneasiness, tension, anger, guilt, anxiety, fear, and pain. These feelings can become an important clue to help you identify your negative thoughts.

Exercise: Connect the Thoughts and Feelings

Think about any bad feelings that you have had recently. Try to remember what you were thinking about at that time and write this down here:

Bad Feeling   **Thoughts**

_____   _____

_____   _____

_____   _____

_____   _____

Characteristics of Negative Thoughts

The first step toward making changes in your negative thoughts is to be able to recognize them. You may be experiencing a pattern of thinking that is markedly different from the way you usually view the world. Ed Bourne described some of the characteristics of negative thinking (Bourne 2000). We'll show how these thoughts may be affecting your life.

You may have these thoughts repetitively and automatically. This means that you have become so accustomed to these thoughts that they seem "normal" to you. You have them instantly and they are easily triggered by everyday events. An example of this might be:

You read about a symphony performance that you would normally love to attend, but you suddenly think of your bad knee and what a nuisance you would be to others in the audience. The words "old" and "crippled" spring into your mind. You forget about going to the symphony.

Because these negative thoughts are so automatic, you do not even think of ways that you could manage to go to the performance. When you are giving your time and energy to negative thoughts, there is little room for more constructive and proactive thoughts. How can you counteract these negative thoughts? Look for solutions rather than problems. You could think about getting tickets with an aisle seat, or getting there early to give yourself plenty of time for seating.

The thoughts are unrealistic. Usually, these thoughts start from a realistic idea but after time, you make generalizations that are actually untrue. This is not to say that your thoughts are delusional, but that you are operating on false assumptions. Here's an example:

A few years ago, you went to a senior center. There were very few people there that day, you ate lunch at a table by yourself, and you had a miserable time. You never went again. A friend raves about her senior center and invites you to go, but you think immediately, "That would be awful. I would have a terrible day. I'm better off staying at home."

Because of your depression and negative thoughts, you draw conclusions without considering all the facts. What are the more realistic thoughts? While it is understandable that your experience was not encouraging, it does not mean that you would necessarily have the same experience again. One day is not enough time to get familiar with a senior center and the people there. It takes time in any situation to get to know people and the schedule. Another fact to consider would be that not all senior centers are alike, and you could very well enjoy your friend's more than the one that you went to.

The thoughts are counterproductive. The negative thoughts influence you to make decisions that will close doors rather than open them. They promote making choices out of fear rather than welcoming opportunity. The result of these thoughts is that you act in a self-defeating manner. You become your own worst enemy. Another example:

A few months ago, you went to the grocery store, and while standing in the checkout line, you tripped and fell. Luckily, you did not get hurt, but you have avoided going to the store as much as you can since. When you do go, you are so distracted by worry and fear that you usually forget to buy the things that you really need. This results in you feeling ineffective and stupid. In fact, you find that you really are frightened of going anywhere, and you feel weaker and less capable every day.

In this situation, one negative experience prevents you from doing ordinary things that you need to do. To counteract this thinking, you can remind yourself of the following: over the years, you have gone to the store thousands of times without falling. The probability that you will fall may be smaller than you think. Even if your doctor tells you that you should be more cautious, there are probably ways that you could still go to the store. You could increase your safety by going with someone else, using a seated cart, or asking the store to gather your items before you arrive.

These thoughts tend to be self-critical and damaging to your self-esteem.
While you may have negative thoughts about other things, most of them center on you. These thoughts fill you with self-doubt and convince you that bad things are happening to you because you are such a worthless person. Consider this:

You go to a family gathering even though you are not feeling very well. Your favorite granddaughter is there with her new boyfriend. You keep hoping that she will come over to you to talk, but she spends less than five minutes with you. You feel very hurt and think, "Why would she want to spend any time with me anyway? I'm so boring and stupid."

One way that you could respond more effectively to this scenario would be to take the focus off of yourself and consider the facts. Your granddaughter has a new boyfriend and may be excited and distracted. She did come over and talk to you. Concentrate on your relationship and how you can communicate your good feelings for her. Perhaps you could call her and spend more time talking. Rather than interpret events to have poor outcomes only, remind yourself of the good that exists.

Is Negative Thinking Contagious?

We hear older adults talk about how depressing it is to go to a senior center or a retirement center and hear only negative stories about other older people's ailments and woes. "Who wants to go to a senior center when everyone there is complaining? I hate going up to someone and asking them how they are and they launch into a long story about how bad their arthritis is." While this may be partly a stereotype about older people (one that should be discarded), it has some basis in truth. Whether you mean to or not, you can communicate your negative thinking to others. You too may have legitimate problems with your health or your life situation. Surely, you should be able to express your thoughts about your problems to others. It's important to be sincere and authentic about your feelings and thoughts. But it is useful to consider whether your problems are the primary topic that you talk about with others. Do you spend more time talking about them than any other subject? Have they overpowered your interest in other matters, to the point of excluding discussion of anything else? It can be hard for other people to respond positively to you if you have gotten into the habit of greeting them with a series of complaints rather than some variety of ideas.

How does negative thinking influence your relationship with those people who are most important to you? Some older adults try to hide their negative thoughts from family and close friends. However, this can inhibit the closeness of your relationships. Other people are unaware of how much they are communicating these distorted thoughts. But people who are close to you know that something is different about you from the changes in your attitude and behavior. Some adult children of older adults have said, "I want to help Dad, but all he can talk about is how bad everything in his life is. What can I do?" Depression can strain relationships and communication. These thoughts can reduce your ability to look outside of yourself and diminish your interest in others. This can result in further isolation.

But there are solutions that will allow you to express your true thoughts and feelings, as well as move toward feeling better. You should spend some time talking with others about what is bothering you. You can do this by arranging a time with a friend or family member or by going to a therapist or a support group. You can talk to your coach. The point is that by becoming aware of when you are talking about these issues, you will be able to control it. One woman we know used the following technique: "I tend to get wrapped up in all the bad things. So I decided to give myself about ten minutes a day to talk to someone about what I am *really* worried about. Then I spend the rest of the time talking about other things—and that does help me feel better."

Exercise: Take a Break

As part of your effort to combat negative thinking, you must spend some of your energy and time thinking and talking about something other than your negative thoughts. A way to look at this is to "take a break" from upsetting thoughts and decide to think about something that offers you some relief and stimulation. What are some topics that interest you? You can practice talking about these topics with other people for at least a few minutes so that you can rest your mind from the burden of negative thoughts. Many people are surprised by how this simple approach can help them restore their good mood, if only for brief periods of time. This can enhance the quality of your social contacts and even help others to challenge their own thinking. Examples of areas of interest are politics, news events, the daily crossword puzzle, movies, novels, and books or sports. Write down your topics of interest here and use this list when you are talking with others:

_____

_____

_____

_____

Self-Esteem and Your "Emotional Anatomy"

Self-esteem is an essential component of your personality and reflects your attitude toward yourself. It may help to think of your self-esteem as a part of your "emotional anatomy." Like a muscle, your self-esteem may have been stronger or weaker at different times of your life. It responds positively to attention and exercise and weakens with continued neglect or injury. Just as changing from a sedentary lifestyle to one of physical fitness takes effort and determination, you will find that nurturing your self-esteem and changing distorted thinking will require work and patience.

Many people go through life without really considering the state of their self-esteem. They might be aware of having bad or good feelings about themselves, but they don't realize that they have the power to do something about it.

Exercise: Your Self-Esteem History

A good place to start with building your self-esteem is to understand it and get some idea of your self-esteem history. Think about a time in your life when you did feel good about yourself and what you were doing. Write down what you remember about that time and what about it helped you feel good:

_____

_____

_____

_____

_____

What Is Self-Esteem?

Some older adults voice concern that having high self-esteem will mean that they have a "big head" or are obnoxious to others. You may have similar worries. The following is a clarification of what self-esteem means in relation to your mental health. Nathaniel Branden (1987) describes what self-esteem is and is not in his book, *How to Raise Your Self-Esteem.* Having a healthy degree of self-esteem is *not*:

- Thinking that you are better or more deserving than other people.

- Expecting that others should suffer for your happiness. Some people have told us they worry that if they start to feel better about themselves, their children or friends will begin to feel bad. This is a distorted belief. Usually, when your self-esteem grows, others tend to respond in a positive way.

- Expecting that others should cater to your demands.

- Exaggerating you abilities when talking with others.

- Being vain.

There are many attributes of self-esteem that are beneficial to your overall well-being. Positive self-esteem *is*:

- Accepting yourself for your good and bad points, and appreciating that there is a balance. Some people have such high standards for themselves that they are continually disappointed. Accepting yourself and your limitations allows you to recognize what you can and cannot change.

- Being able to extend the compassion and understanding that you have for other people to yourself. One of the great truths of life is that we all really do make mistakes. Let those mistakes be a learning experience. When your self-esteem is in good repair, you'll be more able to forgive yourself and move on.

- Being able to enjoy who you are. This is essential for being a confident and capable person.

Your Achievement of Personal Competence

While it can be argued that high self-esteem is not required to succeed in life, it seems obvious that for most of us, our level of achievement and functioning is enhanced when we have positive thoughts about our worth and competence. Personal competence is the sense that you are able to do things adequately for yourself and to live your life. Our society places great value on this concept. A feeling of personal competence allows you to view yourself as a contributing member of society who is worthy of love and happiness.

As an older adult, your view of your personal competence takes on an even greater meaning in terms of maintaining your expectations of independence. No one wants to lose even small parts of his or her independence as an adult. After all, one of the primary tasks that we have as adults is to learn to be independent and we pride ourselves on our ability to do this. There are certainly many older adults who remain independent, throughout their lives. But as we age, the risk of losing some of our hard-won independence increases. Your independence may become a matter of degree rather than something that is absolute. Your level of independence can change as a result of a number of life situations, such as when you sustain an injury, have problems with your vision, are unable to keep up with your yard work, or have difficulty balancing your checkbook.

While some people are at greater risk of losing independence due to medical conditions, it is not always easy to predict whether you will face this in your life. When you are depressed, however, and your self-esteem is low, you may question your abilities unnecessarily. You feel more insecure and more dependent on others. This increased vulnerability is yet another reason why you should become an expert on your own self-esteem and learn ways to build it.

One idea that helps some older adults face the issue of their independence versus dependence is to consider achieving a balance. There will be times in your life when you will be independent and times when you will need to rely on others. When you think about it, even as a younger adult, you were not completely independent in this world. You worked, raised a family, and struggled with problems of everyday living, but you probably had some sort of support from others during your life. And there have probably been numerous ways in which you've helped other people, including friends and family and even people whom you did not know well. You may have a religious orientation or spiritual practice that encourages you to help others in need. Consider that there is a give-and-take in how you help others and how others may help you. You may think of it as part of the circle of life that you have had the opportunity to help others and that you may provide the same opportunity to someone else. It can be an enriching experience for both parties.

This is not to say that you should not strive to be independent. Being as independent as you can in as many aspects of your life as possible is healthy for you and your self-esteem. However, we see many people get into a bind, harming themselves as they try to maintain their independence. Someone who for various reasons can no longer get to the store to buy food should not be trying to exist on a few cans of food saved up in the cabinet. Your overall health can suffer from such a choice. Other people feel ashamed or guilty about getting help. They feel that they do not deserve to have other people pay attention to them. But this is a distortion.

The middle ground between independence and dependence lies in the concept of "interdependence." People who accept their need for others and do not blame themselves for it can handle this with grace and dignity. You do not have to be independent in every realm of your life to be happy or content, but you do need to feel that you are in charge of your life to some degree. You are an individual who is a member of a larger community. In addition to having a family, you are also a part of a larger society. In your lifetime, you have put time and energy and hard work into the building of this society. You learned much about yourself in that effort. Others will learn about themselves when they are able to assist you.

Some older adults have explained how difficult it is for them to ask for help. One woman put it this way: "I know people who have offered to help. But I don't want to become a nuisance. I don't want to be a bother to people. They might think that I am going to expect them to help me all the time." They avoid asking others for help even when they really need it. In fact, the person who puts off asking for assistance when they need it may cause their situation to worsen.

Exercise: Doing It on Your Own

Take a moment to think about your own situation. Write down the areas in which you feel you are dependent on others for assistance. Try to include everything that you can think of and note if this is a temporary or permanent situation. Write down your thoughts and feelings about this dependence:

_____

_____

_____

_____

_____

_____

_____

Exercise: Defining Who You Are

If you are certain of who you are, your need for assistance will not define you. The ways that others may help you does not have to detract from you as a person. You are still the same person inside. You have the same history. You have the same presence. This is crucial for you to come to terms with in order to maintain your self-esteem and dignity, no matter what degree of independence or dependence you are experiencing.

Think about yourself. Write down words and short phrases that describe the characteristics, accomplishments, and good qualities that define who you are:

_____

_____

_____

The standards by which you measure your worth and your competence need to be adjusted at different times in your life. Is it fair to compare your current abilities to the abilities of your earlier self? Many older adults have unrealistic expectations and think they should be able to do things in exactly the same way that they did without effort thirty years ago. You cannot deny that changes have occurred. It may take you twice as long as before to walk around the block. It is not so important that it is taking longer but that you are still doing it. It would be a much greater loss if you were to give up on walking completely just because you do it less well than you used to. It seems pointless to criticize the speed at which you walk when walking can contribute to your general good health.

Marie's Story

Marie's brown eyes sparkle behind her glasses when the subject turns to dancing. "Oh, the music and the orchestras that used to play here. We went to every single performance, Tommy Dorsey, Glenn Miller, all the greats. And everyone was dancing back then. It was marvelous."

Marie, at eighty-three, is often quiet, and she looks at the ground a lot while she talks. But when she talks about those days, she becomes more animated. She talks about her deceased husband and that they were well-suited dance partners, winning contests and going out dancing every week. "Oh, we had so much fun in those days. I love to dance."

Marie's husband has been dead for over twenty years, and Marie has developed arthritis in both knees. She is not a candidate for surgery and now needs a walker to get around. She doesn't like using the walker, and tends to avoid using it. She has a difficult time hearing, but resists using her hearing aids. Over the last few years, Marie has gone out of her home less and less, often doubting why anyone would want to have her company anyway. Eventually she reached a point where she felt sad all the time. "I'm just a tired old lady."

At Marie's low point, her doctor asked her many questions about her mood and outlook and was able to diagnose depression. When Marie went to see a therapist for depression, the therapist encouraged her to try to get reinvolved with activities that had brought her pleasure. Marie's friend Edna asked her to go with her to the senior center, where they had a weekly dance with a seven-piece band. Marie thought that it would just bother her and that she would feel sadder. "Why would I want to go to a dance? I can't dance. I can barely move anymore and I can hardly hear a thing."

Edna finally convinced Marie to join her for "just one time." Marie noticed cynically when she arrived that most of the older folks at the dance were women, and she was prepared to endure one hour of the event and then get a ride home. But she noticed something that she had not expected. As the band played some old familiar tunes, she found herself smiling. She stood up with her walker and tapped her foot gently to the music. Even though her hearing was not great and the band was nowhere near the likes of Tommy Dorsey, it felt surprisingly good to be near it. "I thought that I would be thinking about not being able to get out on that dance floor and show everyone else how to do it. But I really wasn't thinking about that at all, I was just having fun, looking at the other people smiling and moving. It felt so good to be there with the music."

As Marie started working on goals to recover from depression, she realized that she could not bring back the past. Once she discovered this, she was freer to enjoy activities less apprehensively. She became less cynical. Instead of being certain that she would not like something, she found herself more willing to try new activities, such as taking a computer course. She became less critical of herself for not being more like her younger self. "I realized that there are some things about me now that are just fine the way they are."

Taking Charge of Your Self-Esteem

Sometimes there are damaging effects to your self-esteem that come from outside your self, such as a critical parent or an abusive spouse. You may have grown up hearing negative comments about your schoolwork or what you looked like. Many older adults, when they are depressed, hear the abusive words of a parent or teacher who is long gone. Decades seem to disappear and it can feel like moments ago that someone said something angry and critical to you. You forget the many achievements of your life and feel shame and self-doubt. You become sensitive to innocent comments from others and construe them to be pointed at your shortcomings.

But even in the presence of this type of emotional injury, you have the power to strengthen your perception of yourself. Negativity that goes unquestioned is a destructive force to your self-esteem and mood. While other people can support your efforts or influence how you view yourself, it is ultimately in your control to change the habits of your thinking.

Renata's Story

Renata is a sixty-seven-year-old nurse living in a retirement apartment. She had depression several times in her younger life but thought that she was over it. However, she became depressed again following hip surgery last year. As she entered treatment for depression and began working on goals, she became aware that many of her thoughts were returning to the past and the abusive attention that she had received from her father. "My father has been dead for thirty-two years. For the most part, I had shut out my thoughts of him years ago. He was a terrible father to me and my sister, but because I was the oldest, I got the brunt of it." An alcoholic, her father had a terrible temper and had frequent blow-ups centered on all the failings of his wife and children. Renata remembers her father's derisive tone and his cutting comments about her lack of beauty. "He told me that I would never get married because I was so ugly."

In spite of this upbringing, Renata managed her life well. She married and had several children of her own. Before her retirement, she worked as a hospital nurse and received many positive remarks from her patients and supervisors about her exemplary work. Still, when she became depressed this time, she was surprised and discouraged that she began to think so much about the negative remarks that her father had made so many years ago. "Here I am a grandmother, and I'm still thinking about what that horrible man said to me when I was a kid." These thoughts would be triggered when Renata was trying to build her strength doing exercises that her physical therapist had urged her to do. She would think that she was not doing the exercises right and start to doubt if she would ever be able to get better. Then the memory of her father's voice would be in the back of her mind, like a tape recorder, launching in on the attack.

Renata's therapist asked Renata to do an exercise to ease the control that these old criticisms had over her. She asked Renata to write a letter to her dead father—describing herself to him as she really is—to correct his distorted view of her. This was difficult for Renata to do. For a while, she could not get herself to sit down to write. When she finally did, she took a long time in writing the letter. "I let him know all the things that I have done in my life, about my work and my family. I realized that I have a lot to be proud of. At the beginning, I felt scared, but as I wrote, I felt more confident about myself." Renata began to acknowledge that the things that she wrote in the letter were her own true thoughts about herself. "I still have the letter. When I need a little confidence boost, I get it out and read it. Then I remember who I really am."

You will work on exercises and goals to help you move closer to a similar feeling and perception of yourself. Remember, you may not get to that feeling by doing the same things that you were doing before, but these memories hold important clues to what you value and how you might attain self-confidence again.

Exercise: Take a Measurement

It is helpful to measure your self-esteem. A simple way to do this is to rate how you feel about yourself on a scale of 1 to 10. On this scale, 1 means feeling low about yourself and having little or no self-confidence. A 10, on the other hand, signifies that you feel emotionally strong and confident, worthy of feeling happy and content. In the exercise above, for example, at a time when you felt good about yourself, you were probably feeling close to a 10. How would you rate your self-esteem today on this scale of 1 to 10?

Self-Esteem Rating: _____

When you rate your self-esteem on a regular basis, you may find that it changes from day to day. Or yours may be more consistent. It will be important information for you to have about yourself not only for healing, but also for keeping yourself healthy and happy. You will use this tool again in a goal later in the chapter.

Goals for Building Your Self-Esteem and Getting Rid of Those Negative Thoughts

For the goals in this chapter, you will need the assistance of your coach. Many people don't recognize their own negative thoughts, but a good friend or relative will say, "Oh, I know what they are!" They may have been hearing you voice some of those thoughts without you even realizing it. So, open up to this page with your coach and start talking.

Remember your commitment to working on your goals each week. These are things that you need to practice in order to benefit. Making the effort will help you to concentrate better and feel better about yourself.

Goal 9: Identify Your Negative Thoughts

The first step is to identify your negative thoughts and write them down. Remember, you can recognize these thoughts by the fact that you have them over and over and they make you feel bad when you have them. Ask your coach to help you make the list. Write down as many as you can think of:

1. _____

2. _____

3. _____

4. _____

5. _____

Goal 10: Stop Those Negative Thoughts!

A classic tool for fighting negative thinking is to tell yourself to stop having the thoughts. As soon as you become aware of the thought, you must practice alerting yourself to its presence in your mind. Here are several tried-and-true methods. Yes, they sound silly, but even the most cynical people who have actually tried it, swear by it. It works, so give it a shot!

- Place a rubber band on your wrist. When you become aware of a negative thought, snap the band and say "Stop!" out loud. Yes, you can modify this when you are with other people—although it is a great conversation starter and you could get some wonderful support for your effort.

- Find another way to signal yourself that you need to let go of the negative thought. Some people have words that they have chosen, such as "Lighten up" or "I'm okay." Whatever words you choose, try saying them out loud. Share these words with your coach, family, and friends so that they can also signal you to use them when you unconsciously voice your negative thoughts.

Goal 11: Change from Negative to Positive

Once you have identified some of the negative thoughts that you have been having, it is possible to begin the process of reversing them. This process is usually referred to as reframing. Mary Ellen Copeland (2001) recommends in her book, *The Depression Workbook*, to assess your thoughts for the following:

- How realistic is the thought? Negative thoughts tend to generalize, and they tend to include the words "always" and "never." They may be based on something true, but it is unlikely that the negative outcome that you fear is always going to happen.

- Is it deserving of the amount of time that you dwell on it? Negative thoughts are often repetitive and take up a lot of your time.

- Is it overly critical? This can include self-criticism and being overly judgmental of other aspects of your life.

- How much does it interfere with how you live your life? Do these thoughts influence you to avoid trying new things or doing the things that you have enjoyed in the past?

After this initial assessment, you will have a better idea of what your negative thoughts are and how to approach them. One method is to reconstruct or reframe the thought. This does not mean that you must only have happy, Pollyannaish thoughts. Instead, it requires that you find a more realistic and fair way of viewing the thought. Here are some suggestions for you as you reframe your thoughts:

- Be compassionate toward yourself. You may do this by listening to your thoughts. Recognize assumptions that you are making. Here's an example:

    Negative Thought: "I am a worthless person. It's a wonder that anyone would like me."

    Reframe: "I have done many worthwhile things in my life and I am still a worthwhile person. I know that certain people like me very much."

- Accept yourself. Look at the facts and do not judge yourself as good or bad, but simply accept what is. Example:

    Negative Thought: "I can't even climb a flight of stairs anymore. I'm a lazy, good-for-nothing person."

    Reframe: "I can't climb a flight of stairs and for the time being, I will accept it. I can still walk, and if I start walking more, maybe I can get in better shape."

- Forgive yourself. Let go of the past. This does not mean that a wrong is right, but you can let go of it and move on and face the future. Example:

    Negative Thought: "I was a lousy mother. I don't blame my kids for not wanting to see me."

    Reframe: "I made some mistakes as a parent. I can't change the past. But

I am doing what I can now to let the kids know that I love them. I am a good person and I think that will come through."

Take the first three negative thoughts that you were able to identify in Goal 9 and reframe them.

1. _____

2. _____

3. _____

Now, read the negative thought and the reframed thought out loud. Repeat the reframed thought several times. Good! Any time those thoughts enter your mind, try to say the reframed message out loud if possible.

Goal 12: Rate Your Self-Esteem

Rating your self-esteem each day will tell you how you are doing. It will also tell you if your efforts are starting to pay off or if you need more work. Every day this week, at about the same time, rate your self-esteem on a scale of 1 to 10 (with 1 indicating low self-confidence or feeling worthless and 10 referring to feeling good about yourself and what you are doing). Use the table below to record your results, and be sure to think about what the numbers mean for you each day.

Monday	Tuesday	Wednesday	Thursday	Friday	Saturday	Sunday
Self-Esteem Rating:	Self-Esteem Rating:	Self-Esteem Rating:	Self-Esteem Rating:	Self-Esteem Rating:	Self-Esteem Rating:	Self-Esteem Rating:

After assessing your self-esteem for a week, look at the numbers closely. Do you notice any trends? On the days when your numbers were lower, what were you doing? And, more importantly, what were you doing on the days when your numbers were higher? This is good information that should tell you what you should do more of or less of. Talk with your coach about your findings and how you can do more of the things that helped your self-esteem to grow. Write down the answers to these questions here:

Goal 13: Building on Good Feelings

This is a goal that will take some time to think about, so dedicate some time to doing it well. One way to increase self-esteem is to try new things and enjoy them. All too often, an older adult with depression will talk themselves out of personal growth opportunities with the deadly words, "I can't do this or I can't do that." Think about whether you've heard yourself saying or thinking those words. If so, you must reject this self-defeating attitude.

Do you honestly believe that you have done all the growing that you can do? Then a shift in perspective is in order, because an essential component of being alive is growing and learning. As Edmund Bourne points out in his book *Beyond Anxiety & Phobia* (2001), you may be questioning what your life purpose is. While this is a healthy question for you to be considering at this time in your life, depression may be unfairly leading you to only negative conclusions. In reflecting on your life purpose, consider the following questions. Answer them according to your true feelings, not based on what you think you may or not be able to do.

In your lifetime, you may not have been able to do all the things that you wanted to do or thought that you would be good at. Are there any special talents or skills that you have not been able to explore? (Bourne 2001) Is there something that you have longed to do but have not? In what way could you express this in your life now?

Imagine that there are no barriers to the things that you would like to be doing with your life. Make a list of skills or activities that you would like to develop at this time in your life. Consider all areas of interest, including working, pursuing hobbies, volunteering, going to museums, and traveling:

1. _____

2. _____

3. _____

4. _____

5. _____

Now, think about what is holding you back from doing these activities. What are some of the solutions that you and your coach can come up with to eliminate or decrease the barrier that is standing in your way? Concentrate on one barrier and one solution.

Barrier   **Solution**

_____   _____

_____   _____

_____   _____

What are you willing to do in the next two weeks to resolve the barrier? Write down what you can commit to doing, and do it:

_____

_____

_____

Goal 14: Compassion Toward Yourself

Consider kindness that you show toward other people. Too often, when your self-esteem is low, you think of yourself in an unkind way, and this is reflected in how you treat yourself. By showing compassion to yourself, you are building self-respect, not self-pity. Think of ways that you can be more compassionate toward yourself. Your goal is to fill in the following blank and then carry out your promise to yourself.

Today I will show compassion to myself. I will do this by:

_____

_____

_____

Goal 15: Sharing with Others

When you share with others, it can have a positive effect on your own self-esteem. In what ways, however small, do you feel that you could make the world a better place? (Bourne 2001). What could you do to make the world a better place, starting next week? This could include a variety of activities, such as calling someone who is alone, writing a letter to someone in need, volunteering at a hospital, going to visit someone who cannot leave their home, or helping your grandchildren with their homework. Write down all of your ideas here, and then choose at least one thing to do:

_____

_____

_____

_____

Goal 16: Positive Affirmations

Positive affirmations are positive statements that you will say to yourself to focus on your good attributes, skills, and personal qualities. They are very useful for people with low self-esteem to build their belief in themselves and direct their thoughts more productively. Instead of accepting negative, critical self-talk, you can take an active stance and strengthen your self-confidence and determination. Affirmations can help you shake self-doubt and criticisms. They're a way of practicing being assertive with yourself. Your goal is to say at least one positive affirmation to yourself each day. Examples of positive affirmations are:

"I am intelligent and capable of making my own decisions."

"I can get better one step at a time."

"I am strong enough to make it through this."

Now, build some positive affirmations of your own. Write down at least three:

1. _____

2. _____

3. _____

You can be creative with what you do with your positive affirmations. Some people write them down on a small piece of paper and carry them in their wallet or purse in order to look at them periodically. Others tape them to the mirror and practice saying them aloud whenever they see them. Share your affirmations with your coach. Then, have your coach mail a written list of your affirmations to you at some point when you are not expecting it. That way, your own thoughts can brighten your day and your outlook. Keep in mind that they will not have much of an effect unless you are willing to say them aloud or read them regularly.

Strengthening your self-esteem and managing your negative thoughts will take time and effort. But if you work on this every day, you will feel better, stronger, and more capable of taking on life.

Chapter 5

How Grief and Loss Can Help You Grow

Loss is an inevitable part of life. Preparing yourself to cope with the emotions that accompany any loss will help you develop a more compassionate attitude toward yourself and others. Distressing, difficult, and even tragic circumstances can be opportunities for growth.

Richard's Story

Richard is a seventy-six-year-old man with a wry sense of humor and an easy smile. Richard and his wife, Mary, were able to retire comfortably. They had saved and planned for a life together that included traveling, entertaining, and visiting with family and friends. Mary grew up in Denmark but left there at age eighteen to attend college in the United States at the University of Minnesota. She and Richard met in college and were married shortly after they both graduated.

Richard and Mary had four children and through the years had a good marriage and close relationships with their children and the three grandchildren who eventually came along. Richard retired from a successful career in public realtions at age sixty-five and he and Mary decided to move to Arizona where it was warmer and they could enjoy many of the outdoor activities that kept them active and healthy. One day, Mary was out for her morning walk and had a massive heart attack, which killed her almost instantly.

Two years later, Richard described what life was like for him: "I have never recovered from Mary's death. I can't believe that our lives were so perfect—that everything was just the way we wanted it, and now my Mary is gone. She is all I can think about. Whenever I see anything that reminds me of her, I cry uncontrollably. I just don't see any reason to go on living without her."

Richard wasn't able to recover emotionally from his wife's death. He had trouble sleeping, lost weight, stopped his outdoor activities, isolated himself in his home, and cried several times a day. Richard's doctor suggested that he might have depression, recommended an antidepressant medication, and urged him to find a therapist he could talk to. During the first three months of therapy, Richard was able to talk about the debilitating pain he felt at having lost his wife. His therapist urged him to express his pain, anger, disappointment, and loss. Richard began to set small goals for himself. Gradually he increased his activity level and forced himself to interact with other people. He started going to the senior center two days a week and met other people who had also lost their spouses. Richard began to feel hope for his future and a reason to go on living. He came to realize that Mary would have wanted him to be happy rather than lose his life to grief.

The Loss-Depression Connection

Loss is experienced throughout your life. You lose innocence, trust, beliefs, physical health, jobs, loved ones, and even dreams. Even your depression can be viewed as a loss. Depression can make you feel cheated out of valuable time. It seems as though some people have more than they deserve of this very personal and intense experience called grief. You may be among those people who have survived many more losses than others, or you may be a person who has had relatively few losses in your life. As you read this chapter, you will notice that many of the exercises apply equally well to your experience of depression and grief, whether you have experienced the other types of loss or not.

As you age, losses can sometimes occur at a frightening pace. Grief is the emotional and physical reaction to loss of any kind. *Bereavement* is the term commonly used to describe the natural response to the death of a loved one. Both these terms describe a variety of emotions and reactions that are part of the normal range of human response to loss.

Thoughts and feelings following a loss can be complicated and intense. Some people have expectations about how they will feel in a certain situation, only to be very surprised to find that the opposite is true. Take the story of Susan, who was a caretaker for ten years for her husband, who had Alzheimer's disease. She expected that when her husband died she would feel an immense relief—not only for herself, but for her husband as well. His suffering would end. When he did die, Susan instead felt an immense sadness that eventually gave way to depression. Two years later, she still did not feel the relief she had so looked forward to. She wasn't able to initiate all the activities she had planned on doing once her husband was gone. Susan was unable to move forward with her life.

Although loss may be painful, it also provides us with the opportunity to grow and deepen our understanding and appreciation of life. This chapter will look at some of the losses unique to the aging process, and the relationship of grief and loss to depression.

Becoming more aware of how aging affects loss will help you to cope better with the grieving process. If you accept the notion that old age is all loss, then that's how you experience it. Instead, you can prepare for the inevitable losses associated with aging by refusing to accept society's stereotypical view of older adults as despairing and lonely people with nothing left to give. As you age, you change—and adaptability will help you with that change.

More and more people are looking at aging as a time to enrich their lives and the lives of others. Knowing what to expect and being prepared to accept responsibility for you emotional well-being will help make the journey easier. Journeys are emotional and intellectual trips that come with unexpected challenges and joy. Pain can often lead to growth and a greater sense of life's purpose.

Note: It is important to recognize that the concept of grief, and even depression, varies greatly among different cultures. Considering the great variety and numbers of different ethnic groups in America, we must acknowledge some of these differences and recognize that Americans have a perspective that is not shared by many other countries and cultures of the world. We need to take care not to judge another person's experience of loss. What may seem inappropriate to one person is completely normal for another.

For example, grief is experienced as a physical response to loss in many cultures. People may experience physical pain, discomfort, and weakness. In contrast, in America grief is normally viewed as a psychological and emotional reaction to loss. Even the concept of death and dying differs greatly among cultures, as does the emotional and physical reaction to it. It is beyond the scope of this book to examine all the cultural differences in responding to grief, loss, death and dying. However, it is important to realize that these differences do exist and are pervasive throughout the diverse social fabric of this country. The concepts and suggestions that we make in this chapter will be from a predominately American point of view. If you have a different view on how to handle your grief, do what you can to adapt the exercises we provide to fit your needs.

Phases of Grief

Generally speaking, and making exceptions for cultural differences, most individuals of any age go through the same phases of grief after losing a loved one. However, not everyone has all these responses, and they do not necessarily occur in a particular order.

- **Shock**
  You feel confused, disoriented, and unemotional. The reality of the loss has not sunk in.

- **Disbelief**
  You can't believe this is really happening to you. You may even deny the reality of the loss.

- **Emptiness**
  There is an overwhelming sense of sadness and loneliness. All of the support from friends and family has dwindled and you are left alone with your emotions.

- **Confusion**
  You have difficulty concentrating and attending to things. You are forgetful and absentminded.

- **Numbness**
  You know there are intense emotions, but they seem oddly disconnected from you. You are unable to cry.

- **Free-Floating Anxiety**
  You are anxious and overwrought. There are times when you feel like you are going crazy.

- **Anger**
  You are angry with yourself, other people, or God. You don't understand how this could have happened to you.

- **Guilt**
  You blame yourself for something you wish you had done or not done.

Wisdom Is Not All That Comes with Age

Let's take a look at some of the losses that can occur when you are younger, but are more closely associated with getting older. Compare losses in your earlier years to what it feels like to have a loss now. Each type of loss listed below is followed by an example.

Loss of a Loved One

This could mean the death of a spouse, partner, child, friend, or relative. It could also refer to the estrangement of someone important in your life whom you have lost contact with, or a spouse who is diagnosed with Alzheimer's disease and is no longer the same person that you once knew. Loss of a loved one is one of life's most stressful events. It is estimated that about 15 to 25 percent of bereaved individuals show signs of major depression (Hales 1995). So the chance of experiencing a depression following the loss of a loved one is relatively high.

Example: Jean is very close to her two grandchildren and has spent much of her time raising them while her divorced daughter works during the day. She feels they are almost like her own children. Jean's daughter starts seeing a new man who is eventually transferred out of state for his work. Jean's daughter decides to uproot the grandchildren and go with him. Jean doesn't think it is a good idea to take the children away from family and feels betrayed by this decision. There is a hole in her life that can't be filled.

Loss of Physical Health

You may experience physical changes or problems that limit your activity level. An acute or chronic illness may impact your ability or desire to fully participate in life.

Example: Bill has been active his whole life. As he has gotten older, he continues to walk, play golf, and swim. At age seventy-five he has a stroke that leaves him with partial paralysis of his right side. Although he is able to recover much of the functioning he loses as a result of the stroke, he continues to feel weak and has difficulty returning to his previous level of activity. He is devastated by his inability to keep up with his friends during their morning walk and is ashamed to play golf anymore.

Loss of Social Status or Role

You may have had a job or career that gave you a sense of responsibility and importance or kept you busy and active. Perhaps your role as a parent or even a caregiver made you feel appreciated and loved.

Example: Pat was an accountant for a law firm for over twenty years. She was pressured to retire at age sixty-five even though she wanted to keep working. She says, "I just don't know what to do with myself now that I am retired. People appreciated and respected me at work and now that I am home all day, I feel worthless."

Loss of Home

Many older adults leave their homes to live in retirement communities or assisted living facilities. Although this may be positive in many ways, it can be a significant change that causes unexpected feelings of sadness and regret.

Example: José lost his wife two years ago and has become increasingly isolated in the home that he and his wife had lived in together for over fifteen years. José's children have suggested that he would do better to sell the house and move into a retirement community where he would be around other people and have planned activities. After much thought, José decides to do as his children suggest and sells his home. Although the retirement community is very nice and the people friendly, José misses his home. He misses all of the things in their house that remind him of his wife and their life together.

Loss of Independence

This may mean that you are unable to completely take care of yourself, your house, or your spouse. Independence can also mean having the freedom to go where you want when you want. Lack of transportation may mean relying on other people to take you places.

Example: Max has driven since he was fourteen. At age eighty-five he is diagnosed with macular degeneration and gradually begins to lose part of his eyesight. Max's doctor requests that he give up his driver's license for safety reasons. One of the many activities that Max enjoyed is going to the senior center to play pool with "the guys." Now that he can't drive, Max must call for transportation to the senior center, and he can't play pool any longer.

Loss of a Pet

A pet can be a significant source of companionship and comfort. Losing a pet can be a devastating experience.

Example: Nadine is sixty-three years old and has had her dog, Lucky, ever since she rescued him from the animal shelter twelve years ago. "He is all I've got since my husband died two years ago." When Lucky dies of natural causes, Nadine is heartbroken and depressed. She feels as though she has lost a member of her family.

Loss of Financial Independence or Stability

Some older adults may have to rely on limited finances after retirement. Women in particular are sometimes left in a position of having to live on social security alone, without other sources of income. Unexpected expenses can impact long-term financial stability.

Example: Pauline had been married for over forty-five years when her husband, Jack, died following surgery. He always took care of their expenses and paid all the bills. When Pauline assumes their financial responsibilities, she is shocked to discover that Jack had taken out a second mortgage on the house and that there are bills that have gone unpaid. Pauline is now in a situation where she must pay all the bills on the limited amount she gets from their combined social security.

Loss of Social Support System

Social support is fashioned from years of involvement in a variety of endeavors, including work, family, church, and community. Retirement signals the end of work; families move away or get wrapped up in their own lives; neighborhoods change as older residents die or move on to other housing; close friends begin to die; the loss of a spouse makes it difficult to engage with other people.

Example: Bob worked for thirty-five years for the same company. He retired at age seventy and suddenly doesn't know what to do with himself. His wife died three years ago, but he somehow managed pretty well. He had his work to keep his mind off his pain, and keeping busy made him feel productive. Now, Bob is faced with a life devoid of work and his wife. It begins to dawn on him that he hasn't really made an effort all these years to get to know people.

Exercise: How You've Experienced Loss

Try to think about three losses in the context of how they have helped to shape who you are. With every loss, there is something that you gain and ways in which you grow. Although we will discuss how grief can help you grow later in this chapter, start now by writing down the ways you have grown or what you have gained through your losses.

1. My loss: _____

What I gained or learned: _____

_____

2. My loss: _____

   What I gained or learned: _____

   _____

3. My loss: _____

   What I gained or learned: _____

   _____

Many older adults who experience losses are able to move on in positive directions and have a "capacity to develop new adaptive strategies" (Department of Health and Human Services 1999, p. 8). However, some people struggle with the many changes that occur with aging. It's hard to adequately prepare yourself for the shock and pain that accompany the stress of loss, but we will discuss some ways to cope with these troubling emotions in this chapter.

How Aging Intensifies Your Grief

Getting older does not necessarily mean you will have more difficulty coping with grief or that depression is more likely to occur with your grief. However, there are some important characteristics of aging that complicate the grieving process.

- Loss of a spouse is more common in late life. The Surgeon General's Report (Department of Health and Human Services 1999) states that about 800,000 older Americans are widowed each year. Losing a spouse or partner is devastating at any time in life, but as you age, other complicating factors can make it even more difficult to recover from this loss.

- Medical problems more closely associated with aging can make losses more stressful. Imagine that you have a heart condition or high blood pressure and incur a loss. Or perhaps you have something as simple as the flu or a sinus infection. Illness of any kind weakens the body and compromises emotional strength and resolve. The extra stress of a loss can be amplified when there is illness present.

- Enduring a significant loss without adequate social support can make it more difficult to find someone to talk to who can offer you comfort, help, and guidance. Trying to "go it alone" can lead to loneliness and increasing isolation.

- Thoughts of death and mortality may be more likely to occur as you get older. These may be troublesome thoughts for some of you. Perhaps you are fearful and apprehensive about your own mortality and haven't come to terms with these thoughts.

- Regrets and unresolved issues may be accentuated by loss. Loss of a spouse, friend, or relative may give rise to things not said or conflicts not resolved. This can lead to guilt, shame, and regret. Glimpses of your own mortality may bring up feelings of not having accomplished something, or not having been a "good enough" parent, spouse, or friend. Retirement may lead to thoughts of not having been all you could have been. A woman who gave up a career to raise a family may wonder if she missed an important opportunity in her life.

Assessing Your Coping Skills

Self-assessment is an exercise in taking a good, hard, honest look at yourself and how you are coping with grief, loss, or depression. Many of the feelings and behaviors we talk about below can be normal responses to grief and loss, but keep in mind that they should be temporary. Although there is no established length of time to grieve, eventually the feelings subside. It's normal to engage in unhealthy behaviors from time to time, but you should look out for behaviors that persist to the detriment of your ability to move on with your life in a healthy way.

One of the emotions that may be contributing to your difficulty in coping is forgiveness. When you experience loss, regardless of what that loss is, the concept of forgiveness is certain to come up. When something unexpectedly painful arises, we tend to blame someone for our hurt. Most often we end up blaming ourselves for things gone wrong, disappointments unexpressed, thoughts and feelings that were left unsaid, and mistakes that were made. Other times we blame someone else for having "caused" us pain.

In either case, it is important to work on forgiving yourself or someone else for those things that are now past and can't be changed. It can be helpful to talk with your coach, therapist, or someone else who can give you objective feedback on your feelings.

Sarah's Story

Sarah endured an abusive marriage for thirty years. Her husband was controlling and emotionally cruel, but Sarah didn't want to leave him until the children were grown and on their own. She adapted over the years to a very difficult environment and put aside many of the things that were important to her, including a lifelong desire to get a college degree.

After her children had moved out, Sarah finally found the courage to divorce her husband. She was concerned about the financial ramifications of such a decision, but decided that with the help of her family, she could manage without him.

Once her husband was out of the house, the resentment and anger Sarah had felt all those years came to the surface. She blamed her husband for what she felt were wasted years. She had given up so much of her own life.

As time went on, Sarah's anger turned inward as she came to realize that she had made the choice to stay at home and raise her family before leaving her husband. Now she was alone, and she felt responsible for all those lost years. Sarah's anger gave way to a terrible sadness, and the relief she expected never came. Her children urged her to see a counselor who specialized in grief and loss.

As Sarah spent some time with a counselor, she came to understand that she needed to forgive not only her husband, but also herself. She began to realize that it was her responsibility to make the life that she wanted, starting today. There was nothing she could do to change what had already happened. Sarah made all her decisions based on what she believed was the right thing to do at the time, and now it was time to move on in new directions.

Despite the fact that she was sixty-seven, Sarah decided to go back to school and get her college degree. She was able to take classes for free because she was over sixty-five, and in time she earned her bachelor's degree. She never got over the hurt of all those years, but she gained a life that was of her own making.

Exercise: Your Experience with Grief and Depression

Look at the questions below to help you fairly assess how you are handling your grief or depression. Don't be afraid to be honest.

Read each question and circle the best answer:

1. I increasingly spend more time alone. I avoid other people.   Yes   No

2. I am keeping my thoughts and feelings to myself.   Yes   No

3. I feel angry and/or resentful toward other people.   Yes No

4. I am engaging in negative coping skills and/or addictive behaviors, for example: drinking too much alcohol, eating too much, or taking too many prescription medications.   Yes No

5. I have thoughts of wanting to die, or I feel guilty about being alive.   Yes No

6. I spend much of my time blaming myself or someone else for my pain.   Yes No

7. I am having difficulty keeping my place of residence neat and clean.   Yes No

8. I have less and less desire to bathe and keep my clothes laundered.   Yes No

9. I am having trouble paying my bills.   Yes No

10. I feel increasingly guilty or ashamed.   Yes No

11. I feel hopeless about the future.   Yes No

Take a close look at how you answered these questions. Your "yes" answers will give you some insight into how you are coping and what you may need help with. All of your "yes" answers are part of the *process* of grieving and are not necessarily an indication that your coping method is unhealthy. If you are in doubt about how well you are coping, seek the help of a mental health professional.

What To Expect and How to Cope

Many excellent books have been written about the grieving process and the normal emotions associated with it. Most people agree that grieving is a very individual process with no clearly defined time frame. There are numerous books on the grieving process that you may want to read. We will list several of these books in the resources section at the end of the book.

Dale Lund (1996), a professor of gerontology at the University of Utah, offers these suggestions for older adults going through a grieving process:

1. **Never accept the stereotype that later years are less valuable than earlier years.** If you believe that the years you have left (and there are probably many more of them than you think there are) are not valuable, then you won't make wise and healthy decisions. Make a commitment to be the best you can be, and work at creating quality in your life every day. Expect that you will use the same fighting spirit you had when you were thirty to combat your grief and your depression now.

2. **Do not expect your grief to follow an orderly progression. Many people never get over a loss—they just learn to live with it.** Recognize that some pain lasts a lifetime but that life goes on in meaningful ways. Expect setbacks and sorrow even as you start to move on with your life. People may pressure you to have completed certain "tasks" of grieving before you are fully ready or able to do so. Progress in your own way. Just as you can learn to manage your depression, you can manage your loss and the grief that accompanies it.

3. **Remain socially connected and active, and take one day at a time. Set small, practical goals each day.** Use your time in meaningful ways. By staying socially active you will feel more connected to life. It won't be easy, but being around people will give you support and comfort and they too have most likely experienced some grief along the way. We have learned in other chapters how important small goals are in recovering from depression. You have also learned the importance of social connections in improving and maintaining the quality of your life. The same holds true for grief.

4. **Take responsibility for your own adjustment process.** No one can do the painful work of recovering from grief or depression for you. You will have help, but ultimately you are the only one who can make the changes necessary to grow and move on. Accepting the challenge will help you grow and gain self-confidence.

5. **Become more competent in the tasks of daily living. Take the time and energy to cope with losses by learning the daily tasks necessary to stay active and independent.** Refer back to your self-assessment in "Your Experience with Grief and Depression." You may neglect such self-care activities as taking a daily bath and keeping your house clean. Although you may not feel like keeping up with these activities, do so anyway. Declining health and the ability to manage independently can slip precipitously without your even being aware of it. Take responsibility for your own health and well-being. Sometimes losing a spouse or partner can leave you responsible for chores or activities you are not familiar with.

Take the time to learn how to manage your own affairs and ask for help if you need it.

6. **Express your thoughts and feelings.** Don't keep your feelings bottled up. Find a friend or group who will listen and understand. Family members may not always be patient with your grieving process because they are having trouble moving forward themselves. If you can't find someone you are comfortable talking to, start a journal and write your feelings down or tape-record them. When you have depression, even a small loss may become amplified. It's important to acknowledge the intensity of the feelings associated with the loss. Find a grief group if you can.

In addition to the excellent suggestions made by Dr. Lund, there are some other ways to cope with stress in your life. These activities will help with depression also.

- **Take a recess from your grief and relax your mind.** It's okay to give yourself permission to take a break from your grief.

- **Take a hot bath.** This simple practice relaxes your mind and body.

- **Call a friend and talk about something important to that person.** Taking your mind off your troubles can help you put things in perspective. Other people have problems too and could use some support.

- **Treat your body to something special: a massage, pedicure, facial, or haircut.** Indulge in an activity that makes you feel good about yourself and gives you a fresh outlook on life.

- **Rent or go to a movie that is uplifting and positive.** There's a lot to be gained from a little escape. A positive message can lift your spirits and make you feel hopeful again.

- **Take a close look at your diet. Make certain you have fresh fruits and vegetables in the house to eat.** Making yourself eat healthy foods will help you feel better mentally and emotionally. If you have junk food in the house, you are more likely to eat it. Shop for healthy foods and take vitamins if necessary.

- **Take a walk.** If you are able to, taking a walk does wonders for clearing your head and releasing tension. If you are unable to walk, have someone take you out for a ride in the country, along the shore, or in the mountains.

- **Drink lots of water.** Water is essential to life. Every part of your brain and body needs water to function properly. Even mild dehydration can contribute to fatigue, confusion, and depression. Drink eight glasses of water a day unless it is contraindicated medically.

- **Cut down on alcohol or caffeine intake.** Under stress, you are more likely to reach for substances that may not be helpful or healthy. Monitor your intake of alcohol, caffeine, and prescription medications. It is easy to fall into the habit of drinking to calm your nerves or numb the pain, only to awake the next morning feeling worse than before. Drinking too much caffeine can contribute to nervousness and sleep problems.

Exercise: You Know What Is Best for You

You probably have ideas of your own as well. Think about all the activities and experiences that have helped you cope with stress. Write them down here to refer to when you need them:

_____

_____

_____

_____

_____

_____

How Do I Know If I Need Help?

There is no hard-and-fast rule about the difference between grief and depression, and no way to know absolutely when and if grief has become depression. However, if your grief remains unresolved and you are unable to move on with your life in meaningful ways, you may have clinical depression. Although it may take one person six months to resolve many of the feelings associated with grief, it may take someone else two years to work through that same process. Regardless of how long it takes, if there is little or no relief from the intensity of your grief, it is time to get some professional help. Keep in mind that you may always feel the pain of a loss, especially around the anniversary of the event.

Grief can share many of the same symptoms as depression, and grief can evolve into a depression. Depression and despair are common reactions to important losses, and many researchers believe that bereavement is a risk factor for depression. In some cases a loss and subsequent grief reaction can be the trigger for a depressive episode.

Here are some of the symptoms of depression that are also typical of grief:

- **Withdrawal from other people.** You don't want to be around other people, even when they offer their support and caring.

- **Diminished enjoyment in activities that once gave you pleasure.** You don't feel like engaging in your favorite hobbies or other activities. Or when you do, they are no longer enjoyable and you still feel miserable.

- **Not caring about anything.** Nothing seems important enough for you to be involved. You feel numb.

- **Feeling like there is no meaning to your life.** Your sense of purpose is gone. What use is your life if you are to feel this way?

- **Fatigue.** You are tired all the time, and no amount of rest seems to help.

- **Decreased sexual desire.** You have no desire for intimacy of any kind.

- **Feelings of extreme dependency on other people.** You sometimes feel as though you just aren't capable of doing things on your own. Your sense of self-confidence is gone.

- **Feelings of helplessness.** You feel as though you can't possibly manage independently.

- **Loneliness and sadness.** Although there are people in your life who care about you, you continue to feel alone and despondent.

- **Feeling hopeless.** You just know that you will never feel any better.

- **Feeling that you have been abandoned.** You feel as though no one understands your pain. People who are close to you don't spend the time with you that you need.

- **Shame and guilt.** You feel responsible in some way for the loss, or for the way you are reacting to the loss or situation. You feel badly about not being able to handle your emotions more effectively.

- **Feeling like your life is out of control.** You feel overwhelmed and unable to cope with all the details of life. There is no possible way to get your life back in order.

- **Difficulty concentrating.** You are distracted by your own overwhelming feelings of sadness and despair. Your attention span is limited.

- **Physical problems.** Your entire physical system seems to be out of whack. Your sleep, digestive system, appetite, and energy are disrupted.

Depression may be present if grief persists without some resolution and there is the presence of the following symptoms for a two-month period or longer:

- **Thoughts of your own death.** You would rather not go on living. You feel as if your own death is imminent even though there is no realistic reason for this to be so.

- **Persistent feelings of worthlessness.** You have negative thoughts about yourself. You have problems with your self-confidence and feel incapable of managing your life.

- **Inability to function at your usual level.** You can't seem to get back on your feet. You aren't able to keep up with your bills, your house, and the other parts of your life that need your attention. Social obligations are difficult to cope with; you have trouble working.

- **Difficulty sleeping.** You have trouble getting to sleep or staying asleep, or you wake up too early.

- **Weight loss.** You have no appetite. As a result, you start to lose weight.

Sonia's Story

Sonia is a very pleasant and kind seventy-year-old woman who lives in a middle-class neighborhood in a town in the Midwest. She worked as a schoolteacher for over fifteen years, and she and her husband retired at about the same time when they each turned sixty-five. They have one son, who lives on the East Coast.

Sonia says she has had depression most of her life, but raising her family and working for so many years helped her to manage it well. She has been taking antidepressant medications for several years now, and they have helped her keep her mood on an even keel.

Not long after retirement, Sonia's husband, Dan, began to develop symptoms of Alzheimer's disease. He started to have problems remembering where he lived, what his phone number was, and how to balance the checkbook. His difficulties worsened over the next two years as he became belligerent and more and more confused. Sonia had trouble taking care of him and was often frightened of this man she no longer seemed to know. She was tired all the time and couldn't leave Dan alone for fear he would wander off or leave a stove burner on and start a fire. Their son was unable to leave his job and family to provide any help and suggested that Sonia place Dan in a nursing home for people with Alzheimer's.

Sonia didn't want to put Dan in a nursing home. She was wracked by guilt and indecision, but she also recognized that she could no longer physically care for Dan in his condition. Sonia finally placed Dan in the nursing home. She felt as though he may as well have died, since he no longer recognized her. Her guilt grew with each daily visit. The realization that Sonia had lost her husband began to drain her energy away even more. Any relief at not having to care for Dan was overshadowed by overwhelming loneliness, guilt, and fear for the future. Sonia couldn't sleep well at night and her appetite was almost nonexistent. She knew her health was suffering, but she just didn't care.

Six months after Sonia placed Dan in the nursing home, he died. Sonia began to have thoughts of her own death and wished she could join Dan. Sonia's son suggested that despite the fact that she was continuing to take her antidepressants, her depression had returned and she needed to get help. After repeated pleadings by her son, Sonia finally talked to a friend, who told her about a grief group that met monthly at a local church. She decided to join, and was astonished by how relieved she felt to talk about everything she had been through over the previous three years. With time, she began to feel hopeful about life again and came to understand that she did the right thing with Dan.

How Your Grief Can Help You Grow

The intense emotions that result from a painful experience can turn your world upside down. Routine is disrupted and things can seem unfamiliar and chaotic. Paradoxically, this experience can actually provide some significant and lasting insights about your life. Here are a few of them:

- **A greater appreciation for life.** The pain of grief can help you to appreciate the preciousness of life. Your values and beliefs may come into question, but you come away from the experience with a renewed sense of caring about all that is important to you.

- **A sense of having coped with a difficult challenge and survived.** Coping means not giving up. When you are faced with an emotional battleground and come away having survived that challenge, you are psychologically fortified. You are better prepared to face future challenges.

- **A deeper understanding of your own inward journey.** Loss occurs on so many levels. In an attempt to view aging positively, we sometimes place too much emphasis on the physical aspects of successful aging. We often neglect to consider a person's inward emotional and spiritual journey. Loss often brings up thoughts and feelings on the meaning of life and death and your purpose for being here. It is difficult to capture the inward journey because it is so intangible and personal. Grief can accentuate these feelings and many times pave the way for a deeper understanding of the meaning of life and death.

- **A sense of having confronted your fears.** Many fears arise when you have a loss. Especially as you get older, experiencing one loss may lead you to fear other losses. Confronting and learning to deal realistically with these fears can give you an increased feeling of confidence and control. Fears are only feelings that are attached to an anticipated outcome that may or may not happen.

- **Learning to reach out to others for support, which also teaches you how to offer that same support to others.** Asking for support can be hard. In some cases you may be asking for support that makes you more dependent on someone else. Learning to ask for what you need can help you see how valuable people are to one another. You may increase your awareness of how important it is for you to give others this same support and caring.

- **Better developed self-care skills and resources.** Learning to take good care of yourself when you least feel like it is something to be very proud of. By establishing these good patterns now, you will be able to rely on them for the rest of your life. Stress takes an enormous toll on your body, and if you take the time and make the effort to stay healthy, you will be better able to withstand subsequent stress. In the process of coping with your loss, whether it is the loss of a spouse or loss of functioning, you will discover inner resources you didn't know you had.

- **Recognition that every challenge, transition, and change offers you an opportunity. Find the opportunity in adversity.** If you believe that every hardship has some reward, you will be more likely to experience loss with an open mind and heart. This is not the same as "looking at the world through rose-colored glasses," but accepting and expecting that every loss will have something to teach you. One woman says after she loses her eyesight, "I have been able to do things I never thought possible. I have come to appreciate the little things in life and especially my other senses!"

At the time you are experiencing loss and grief, it may be very difficult to see what good can come of it. But emotional pain is part of being human, and when you realize that everyone goes through it at some time in their lives, you will know that you are never alone.

Moving Forward from Loss

Regardless of what your loss is, having some goals will help you move forward. Many of these are similar to the ones we discuss for depression and can be of help regardless of your circumstances.

Goal 17: Establish Your Support System

You probably already have a larger support system than you realize. Take a moment to list all the supports that you have in your life now. Don't forget to include friends, community organizations, church, family, aging agencies and programs, cultural organizations, and health-care providers.

My support system:

_____

_____

_____

_____

_____

_____

_____

Goal 18: Creating Your Healthy Space

Create a nurturing, healthy, and calming environment. Your environment has a significant impact on your emotional and physical well-being. If the space where you live is chaotic, cluttered, noisy, or not private, you will feel more stressed and less capable of handling crisis.

There are many simple things you can do to create a peaceful, nurturing environment that takes care of you as much as you take care of it. Imagine creating your living space just the way you need it to be without regard to money, time, energy, or space.

My healthy space:

_____

_____

_____

_____

_____

_____

_____

As you take a look at what you have written, choose the things that you can do now, whether it is adding more music, clearing away some clutter, or asking someone you live with to allow you some privacy.

Three things I can do now to improve my environment:

1. _____

2. _____

3. _____

Goal 19: Talking and Writing to Help You Move Forward

Talking helps much more than you think it will. Talking has the effect of releasing some of the pressure that you feel and gives you a sense of perspective on your situation. Choose someone who will take the time to really listen to what you have to say and who you know cares about you. If you aren't comfortable talking, then write daily in a journal.

Goal 20: Identify Your Favorite Hobbies and Activities

When you are stressed, depressed, or grieving, the things that once gave you pleasure seem to have vanished from your mind. Keeping a list of the things that make you feel creative, peaceful, stimulated, or successful can come in handy when you aren't sure what to do next. Don't forget the simple things like taking a walk, listening to music, or buying flowers.

My favorite things to do:

_____

_____

_____

_____

_____

_____

_____

Goal 21: Give the Gift of Giving

Take a step outside yourself and give your time to someone else. You may want to call someone who you know is not doing well, or volunteer to help someone. If you want to do this anonymously, check your local paper and see who needs help. You may choose to simply give a gift to someone.

What I can do to help someone:

_____

_____

Goal 22: Knowing When to Ask for Help

It takes time to heal from the pain of a loss. If you feel that you aren't doing well, ask for help. Call a counselor or clergyperson, or if you have a good relationship with your doctor, talk with him or her.

People I can call for help:

_____

_____

_____

As hard as it is to go through your losses in life, know that you are never alone. Rely upon your friends, family, and community to help you recover and grow. Be open to the possibility of change through pain, and have faith in your ability to move forward.

Chapter 6

Medications

In recent years, medical science has produced a myriad of choices for the treatment of depression with medication. Still, many older adults question whether medication is right for them. Learning about these medications will arm you with the information that you need to make the right choice for you.

Ben's Story

Ben is a bright and active seventy-seven-year-old who works part-time at his son's engineering firm. A few years ago, he had a problem with depression following a stroke. While his rehabilitation went well, he couldn't get over a feeling of sadness and irritability. He felt discouraged and self-conscious and did not seem to enjoy doing his usual activities. "I have a great woodworking shop in the basement. My wife would say, 'Ben, get down there and work on some of your projects. It will help you feel better.' But I would get mad at her and tell her to leave me alone. She told me that I was turning into a real grouch."

Eventually, Ben and his wife talked to their family doctor about the change in his mood and behavior. Their doctor determined that Ben was depressed and suggested an antidepressant. "I was very upset about it. I really don't like to take any kind of pills. After the stroke, it seemed like every time I turned around, someone was pushing another pill at me. But I've known my doctor for a long time and he has always been straight with me." Ben talked it over with his wife and they decided together that it would be worth a try. At first, Ben expected to feel better right away. The first week, he had some mild diarrhea, and he still felt depressed. When he talked to the doctor about this, his doctor told him how the medication would work and that it might take a number of weeks or even a couple of months to really get the best results. He asked Ben to stay on the medication and to let him know if the diarrhea didn't go away in a few days. Ben felt discouraged by this but decided to keep taking the pills and try to keep his mind on other things.

In a couple of weeks, Ben noticed that he was sleeping better. He no longer had problems with diarrhea, and in fact, his appetite was getting better. After about a month, he found that he could talk to his wife more about the things that were irritating him. "Instead of chewing her out, I would try to talk about what was bothering me. She was so glad that I wasn't as grouchy to her." Over time, Ben started going down to his workshop. "I didn't really enjoy it at first. I would just go down and clean up my tools, get things organized. Then I would do a little project here and there. After a while, it started to feel good again."

Ben realized that between the medication, the support of his wife and doctor, and his own decisions to try to do activities that he had enjoyed before, he was getting better. "I feel like the medication gave me an advantage, helped me get out of feeling so depressed more quickly. Now, I'm working for my son and I feel like I am back to my old self."

Antidepressants: Drug Company Hype or Medical Progress?

As anyone who reads the paper or watches television knows, there has been an explosion of new medications and much debate about their effect on our society. Advertising that demands that you "ask your doctor about this pill now!" creates both concern and skepticism in the general public. You may feel that you need something to help you recover from depression, but are uncertain about the effects and safety of these medications. When talking to family or friends, you may hear success stories about how an antidepressant has helped turn someone around from a deep depression. At the same time you may hear speculation about how these pills can cause problems such as weight gain or that they can interact dangerously with other pills that you may be taking. Some reports even claim that these pills can actually change a person's personality. It can be very disconcerting, and it's difficult to know what to believe.

The cost of the newer antidepressants is substantial and may add further to the complexity of this choice. Many older adults on a fixed income and without a supplemental insurance plan simply cannot afford them. As of this writing, the prescription drug benefit for seniors within Medicare is being debated. But even if such a benefit is enacted, it is not likely to cover the full costs for every older adult. Some older adults may still be forced to choose between paying for their heart pills or their antidepressants because they do not have enough monthly income for both. A few of the pharmaceutical companies are responding to the public outcry by trying to produce less expensive forms of their drugs, and almost all of the manufacturers are offering patient-assistance programs that help provide medications to individuals on limited incomes for limited periods of time. More information about this is given later in the chapter.

Our approach will be to encourage you to get as much information as you can in deciding whether or not to take a medication for depression. An informed choice is better than one based on fear, rumors, or lack of knowledge. Because we have seen so many older adults benefit from using antidepressants, we believe that it is an important option for you to consider. At the same time, we have worked with older adults who chose not to take antidepressants. Those people were able to help alleviate their depression by participating in intensive mental health counseling, also known as "talk therapy." There are trade-offs to either decision.

This chapter will discuss the most common concerns about taking medication voiced by the older adults that we have worked with, but will by no means provide all the information that you will need. In order to get the most up-to-date information on drug therapies, you will need to ask questions of your health-care professional regularly. We will present much information to get you started here, but you will also need to consult your health-care professional with your specific questions and concerns.

Exercise: Speak Up!

If you are considering starting an antidepressant to treat depression, write down your greatest concerns here. If you have already been taking a medication for depression, write down any current questions or concerns. Then talk to your health-care provider about these concerns.

How Are the Newer Pills Different

In the 1950s, antidepressants called *tricyclics* were introduced in the United States. These include the brand-name medications Elavil (amitriptyline), Sinequan (doxepin), and Tofranil (imipramine.) They are all effective medications to treat depression and are still used today. The problem with the tricyclics is their higher degree of side effects. We will talk further about side effects in the next section of this chapter.

In the 1960s, another class of antidepressants, the MAO-inhibitors (MAOIs), emerged. These include Nardil (phenelzine) and Parnate (tranylcypromine). Again, these medications are effective in the treatment of depression, but can cause serious and even potentially fatal reactions when combined with some common foods and medications. They are therefore usually reserved for the treatment of very persistent or difficult-to-treat forms of depression.

In 1988, the first selective serotonin reuptake inhibitor (SSRI), Prozac (fluoxetine), was approved for use in the U.S. There are now five SSRIs available including Zoloft, Paxil, Luvox, and Celexa. Additional antidepressants that differ in mechanism of action have more recently been introduced. These include Remeron (mirtazapine), Effexor (venlafaxine), Serzone (nefazodone), and Wellbutrin (buproprion).

After being introduced with much fanfare, the SSRIs were often praised as miracle drugs, because they are far safer and better tolerated than the older tricyclics. It is important to keep in mind that clinical research has consistently shown that the SSRIs are about as effective at treating depression as their predecessors, the tricyclics. In other words, your symptoms of depression will likely improve to the same degree with either category of antidepressant, though a given individual may get a better result from one or the other class of drug.

Side Effects

There is a significant difference in the seriousness of side effects that you might encounter between the tricyclics and the SSRIs. The side effects of the tricyclics are much more troublesome, especially for older adults, than those of the SSRIs. In particular, older adults are more vulnerable to what are called the anticholinergic effects of certain medications. Anticholinergic effects are those that cause drowsiness, dry mouth, constipation, and blurred vision. Other common medications also have anticholinergic effects. For example, many doctors warn you that you should not take certain over-the-counter drugs that are highly anticholinergic, such as Benadryl (diphenhydramine hydrochloride), because of potentially dangerous side effects. In addition to the side effects listed above, anticholinergic medications can also cause symptoms such as confusion, forgetfulness, paranoia, and even hallucinations. If these effects are undetected and the anticholinergic medication is continued, a medical condition called delirium can result. The tricyclics tend to be highly anticholinergic. The SSRIs are not (except for Paxil, but it has very low anticholinergic effects compared to the tricyclics). For this reason, though they are less expensive than the SSRIs, tricyclics are not considered an appropriate first line of treatment for older adults.

This is not to say that the SSRIs do not have side effects or potentially produce harmful outcomes. They do. But for most people, the side effects caused by the SSRIs tend to occur in the first couple of weeks of use and then dissipate. These commonly include drowsiness, headache, and gastrointestinal problems such as diarrhea, nausea, or changes in appetite. Changes in sexual functioning are also possible, such as delayed ejaculation and problems attaining orgasm. Some people notice a brief reappearance of these initial side effects at the time of an increase in the dose of medication. Obviously, if these side effects go from being mild to severe, or persist for more than three to four weeks, your doctor or prescribing professional will want to know immediately and reevaluate the medication.

The following table describes some of the common side effects of the SSRIs and their frequency as reported in the CNS News Special Edition, *Review of Psychotropic Drugs* (Puzantian and Stimmel 2001). *It is important to remember that you may not have any of these side effects, but that they are possible.*

Medication	Sedation	Change in Blood Pressure	Sexual Dysfunction	Gastrointestinal Effects	Restlessness/ Insomnia
Celexa (citalopram)	Low	None	Very high	High	Low
Prozac fluoxetine)	None	None	Very high	High	High
Luvox (fluvoxamine)	Moderate	None	Very high	High	Low
Paxil (paroxetine)	Low	None	Very high	High	Low
Zoloft (sertraline)	Very low	None	Very high	Very high	Moderate

One of the most common problems is with some sort of stomach upset. The likelihood of this can be decreased by eating something around the time that you take your medication, even if it is something small like a couple of crackers with a glass of milk. A very helpful way that side effects can be avoided or minimized during your initial use of medication is by starting with a low dose. Psychiatrists have found that older adults tolerate these antidepressants better when the starting dose is low and dosage increases are made slowly. The rule of thumb is "start low and go slow." While some older adults can get good results in the smaller dose range, you may eventually need the same amount of the drug as a younger adult would to get the best effect. For example, the therapeutic dose of Prozac for adults ranges from 10 to 80 mg daily. As an older adult, your doctor may start you at 5 to 10 mg, but may then need to move slowly up to a higher dose of 40 mg over time to adequately manage your symptoms.

Another important factor is how long the medication will take to start decreasing the symptoms of depression. Unlike taking an aspirin for a headache, you will not experience an immediate relief of symptoms. Unfortunately, it takes a long time for the medication to have its beneficial effect on brain chemistry. In most younger adults taking SSRIs, the length of time to have a noticeable improvement in symptoms can be in the range of four to six weeks. For older adults, this can be as long as eight to twelve weeks, though some start to feel better as early as the first week on a new medication. There is some evidence that one of the newer antidepressants, Effexor, takes less time for improvement in mood to occur. But all of these medications require a great deal of patience for you to continue to take them, day after day, when you are not getting immediate results. It takes a commitment on your part. With time, patience often pays off, and you can feel significantly better.

How Do They Work?

Much has been learned recently about the chemical changes that occur in the brain when depression develops. Serotonin is one of many neurotransmitters, or chemical messengers, that send signals from one brain cell to another. Medical researchers have found that when people are depressed, they tend to have lower levels of serotonin in their brains than when they are not depressed. Additional neurotransmitters, such as norepinephrine and dopamine, are also thought to impact depressed mood.

As more and more people have used antidepressant medications, doctors have determined that they can be helpful to treat more than just depression. For example, in areas of medicine outside of psychiatry, they are used for the treatment of irritable bowel syndrome, migraine headache, and the control of chronic pain. Many of the newer medications also reduce anxiety, which is often present with depression. Specific types of anxiety, such as panic disorder, can be significantly relieved. Many people who have had problems sleeping find their sleep improves with the right antidepressant. Clearly, brain chemistry plays an active role in a variety of clinical problems.

Antidepressants have an effect on the activity level of serotonin and other neurotransmitters in the brain, as explained by Stephen Stahl (1998). These neurotransmitters are chemical messengers that carry signals from one brain cell, or neuron, to the next. The SSRIs in particular influence serotonin activity. By altering the processing of this brain chemical between brain cells, more serotonin is made available for use. Other types of antidepressants, such as Remeron and Wellbutrin, influence the activity and levels of serotonin, as well as additional neurotransmitters, norepinephrine and dopamine, by a variety of other mechanisms.

Most medications have a "half-life" or an amount of time that the major active ingredients are available to work in your body before they are inactivated. Older adults process medications more slowly, and active ingredients can stay in your system longer than in a younger adult. Most of these medications have a relatively short half-life, meaning that they are out of your system within a day or so. The exception is Prozac. Prozac has the longest half-life of any of the antidepressants and has recently come out in a form that can be taken once a week, which is enough for some people to achieve a full antidepressant effect. But generally, you cannot skip taking an antidepressant for a couple of days and expect it to continue to work properly.

What About Other Medications?

Modern psychiatric practice uses a wide variety of drug therapies for depression that includes many different drugs. Your doctor or health-care professional may prescribe more than one antidepressant at one time or add a "mood stabilizer" medication to a standard antidepressant. An example is Depakote (valproic acid). The mood stabilizers are pills that are used primarily for another form of depression called bipolar disorder (as described in chapter 1). Recently, these mood stabilizers have been found to help treat depression and anxiety even when bipolar disorder is not present. Your doctor might also prescribe an anti-psychotic medication such as Risperdal (risperidone) or Zyprexa (olanzapine) to help with depression or anxiety. Although these medications are used primarily for the treatment of psychotic disorders such as schizophrenia, they can be useful in small doses for older adults with more difficult-to-treat forms of depression.

Some older adults ask us about other medications that they may have been taking for a long time, with the assumption that these other pills are also for depression. For example, people will tell us they've been taking prescription medications called benzodiazepines for years. The benzodiazepines include Valium (diazepam), Serax (oxazepam), Ativan (lorazepam), Xanax (alprazolam), Klonopin (clonazepam), and others. Some people think of these as their "nerve pill" or as a sleeping pill. In fact, the benzodiazepines are indicated for the treatment of anxiety, not for depression. While they do cause sedation and may be used for a limited time to help you sleep (the night before surgery, for instance), they are not meant to be used for that purpose in an ongoing way. In fact, research has shown that this class of drug can disrupt quality sleep if used over a long period of time.

When used for the treatment of anxiety, the benzodiazepines can be quite useful. They act rapidly and aid people who are experiencing severe anxiety to feel better quickly. For people who have occasional bouts of intense anxiety, their doctor may prescribe this type of drug for intermittent use. Some people with very persistent forms of anxiety may even need to take these medications on a daily basis.

Generally speaking, however, the benzodiazepines should be used conservatively. The major concern for many people with this type of medication is that it is addictive, both mentally and physically. Psychological addiction does not happen with every person who takes this type of drug, but it can happen. Some people become accustomed to the euphoria or "feeling good" response to the drug, and this can lead them to take more than prescribed. In addition, as the drug moves out of your system, it can cause you to experience an increase in anxiety, the very reason that you started to take it in the first place. This makes it especially hard for people who have been taking these pills for years to discern whether they are having a return of their original anxiety or a withdrawal reaction to the absence of the drug. And, if you suddenly stop taking these medications, as opposed to a gradual tapering of the dose, you can have symptoms of withdrawal, which if not managed medically can result in seizures and even be fatal.

There are additional concerns with benzodiazepines if you are an older adult. Some hazardous responses to these medications can occur. Benzodiazepines affect your central nervous system and can cause adverse reactions in older adults. Your reaction time can slow; you may be more forgetful and confused. In addition, this type of pill can cause dizziness and impair your coordination. Benzodiazepines can be a factor in falls and their related injuries among older adults. They can even intensify or cause depression in some people.

In spite of the hazards, many people are reluctant to give up these pills. Some people think of them as a source of comfort. You may even think of the medication as an old, reliable friend that has helped you sleep. You may be someone who has a legitimate need for these medications. But for your overall health and safety, it is imperative that you discuss them with your doctor. You and your doctor should consider your situation and your symptoms. If you and your doctor believe that it is in your best interest to continue to use a benzodiazepine, then you should be using the lowest dose that is effective for you. You should review your use of this type of drug regularly and consider what alternatives might be available.

Noreen's Story

Noreen is a petite and vivacious sixty-nine-year-old woman who lives with her husband, Jack. Her once jet-black hair is now a becoming silvery gray, and

Noreen enjoys getting a new hairstyle now and then. "It perks me up to have a little change of pace." Noreen is interested in the history of her town and is a member of a local historical society. She and Jack enjoy walking and fishing together.

During her younger adult life, Noreen had been married to another man. The marriage was not a happy one and by the time they divorced, Noreen had had her first bout of depression. She was forty-two at the time. "I was so depressed and crying all the time, I could hardly make it to work. That was when my doctor first prescribed Valium for me. It really helped calm me down. Somehow, I started back to work."

Even after her depression had passed, Noreen kept taking the Valium, mostly at night to help her sleep. Sometimes if something at work really upset her, she would take an extra one. "I started carrying them in my purse, you know, for security. I just felt better knowing that they were there if I needed one." When she was fifty-seven, Noreen was in a car accident that left her with a limp and chronic pain in her hip. She ended up retiring early. "The pain pills never seemed to help. By that time, my doctor had switched me from Valium to Ativan. I thought that the Ativan was better for me than the Valium. If it wasn't for the Ativan, I wouldn't make it through the day. I just dreaded the pain coming on." Noreen noticed that she was taking more and more Ativan just to counteract the worry and the pain. She became depressed again and went to her doctor for help. He prescribed an antidepressant. It helped for a while but then the depression got worse. Noreen began to think about suicide. "I just wanted to be numb. I wanted the pain to go away." Noreen would take enough Ativan so that she could sleep through much of the day.

Two years ago, a neighbor of Noreen's found her one day on her couch, slurring her words and unable to make sense. The neighbor called an ambulance and Noreen was admitted to a psychiatric unit at the hospital. "The psychiatrist was a very kind man. One day, he held my hand and looked me in the eye and told me that I was taking too much Ativan, and that I was addicted to it. He explained that it was making it harder for me to get over depression. I felt angry and scared, but what could I do? I knew he was right. I knew that something had to change." The doctor slowly tapered down Noreen's dose of Ativan over several days and monitored her vital signs to make sure that she was not going into withdrawal. He started her on a new antidepressant. Noreen attended group therapy. She continued group therapy after she left the hospital and also attended AA meetings to help her understand the addiction process and how it had prevented her from using healthier coping skills.

Noreen met Jack at AA; they were married six months ago. He has been a strong supporter for her recovery from addiction to Ativan, as well as her recovery from depression. Noreen now has a different outlook on her life. "I think that the psychiatrist at the hospital saved my life. I was convinced that I would not be able to cope with the pain without the Ativan. But I don't know where I would be now if I hadn't stopped taking it. I still have a great deal of pain. But I deal with it. I can do so much more with my life."

Alternative Medicine: Is It Better?

The interest in alternative medicine has grown tremendously in recent years. Many people are looking for simpler, more "natural" solutions to health problems. Some people believe that by using something natural, the medication will be safer and that there will be less danger of side effects. This is not always the case. Natural medicines made from plant products often contain potent chemical compounds whose effects on the body must be taken as seriously as any traditional drug.

Your choice of alternative medicine is complicated by the fact that they are produced by a largely unregulated industry and the composition and quality of the products can vary widely from one manufacturer to another. While the alternative treatments for depression usually cost less than their traditional counterparts, you can still spend quite a bit of money on them. Beware of extravagant claims of cures and miracles. Many alternative medicines on the market today have not been researched adequately for their safety and effectiveness.

There is much debate about the usefulness of alternative medicine approaches. Of those alternative medications that have been tested, the results can be conflicting. This can make your choice for using these drugs more confusing. An example of this is the scientific research concerning St. John's Wort. St. John's Wort, derived from a flowering bush, is often used for the treatment of depression. It is widely marketed in a variety of forms and strengths, including pills and teas. St. John's Wort affects the activity of the neurotransmitter serotonin in the brain. It is thought to do so less powerfully than the SSRIs. Much research about St. John's Wort has been done in Europe, where alternative medicine is widely practiced. There is a body of research to verify its effectiveness. However, a recent study published in April 2001 in the *Journal of the American Medical Association* (Shelton, Keller, et al. 2001) found that St John's Wort was not effective for the treatment of depression. Because of prior research that indicated otherwise, further studies are needed.

Because of its effects on brain chemistry and potential to interact with other medications, it is essential to discuss your use of this drug or any other "natural" remedies with your physician. Some people want to take St. John's Wort or other alternative medications at the same time that they are taking prescription antidepressants in the hopes that it will increase the benefit. However, there is some concern that this could dangerously elevate the level of serotonin. Consult your doctor or health care professional before combining St. John's Wort or any alternative medicine with any other drugs.

Why Should I Take Medications?

By now you have read a lot of complex information about medications. It can be a bit overwhelming to learn all you need to know to make informed choices. Whether you are already taking medications for depression or are currently making your decision, it is clearly a big responsibility. We have divided some common reasons that people choose to take antidepressants into those that are reasonable and those that are unwise—the "good" and "bad" reasons. Here are a few of each:

"Good" Reasons to Take Medications for Depression

- You can start feeling better sooner. While you may balk at the idea of waiting eight to twelve weeks for an antidepressant to be maximally effective, you may be one of the many people who begin to feel relief from some symptoms within the first few weeks. As each symptom decreases, you will feel gradually better. Without medication, the symptoms could stay the same or get worse.

- By taking an antidepressant, you can decrease your symptoms to the point where your depression is largely controlled. Some people will attain a complete remission of all symptoms of depression, and the majority of people treated with antidepressants feel better than before they took them.

- By combining medication with psychotherapy, you have a greater chance of feeling better. You may have tried counseling and found that you still feel significantly depressed. Recent scientific studies have shown that the combination of therapy and antidepressant medication is even more effective than antidepressant medication taken alone or psychotherapy alone to combat depression. Taking antidepressants can give you an excellent advantage if you are in therapy as well.

- Antidepressants can help restore the balance of sleep and energy. Many older people have problems with sleeplessness and fatigue that are compounded by depression. In some cases, the newer antidepressants can eliminate the need for additional sleeping pills by regulating sleep and energy. And they are generally safer to use than the older sleeping pills.

"Bad" Reasons to Take Medications for Depression

- "Medications can make life easy." Antidepressants can help decrease your symptoms, but they cannot change your life. Life is inherently difficult and you will always experience times of stress. If you are less depressed, however, you are more likely to use coping skills more effectively to manage tough times.

- "The pills will help me feel good all the time." Antidepressants are designed to decrease the negative symptoms of depression. They will not provide a "high" or elevated feeling. It is important to have realistic expectations of what medications can do for you.

- "My doctor/family member is pressuring me to take medications, so I guess I will have to do it." While in some cases this may be a "good" reason to take medication, is more likely that you will have a better outcome with antidepressants or any therapy when you have made your own choice to do it. If you resent taking medication, you may find ways to sabotage the results by not taking them as directed.

Exercise: Know Your Expectations

What are the reasons that you are taking or considering taking a medication for depression? What are your expectations about what medications can do for you? It may help you to clarify your thoughts about this by writing down your reasons here:

_____

_____

_____

What Kind of Pill-Taker Are You?

When you make the decision to take medication, you are also making an agreement to take the pills the way the doctor or health professional instructs you to. This is true for any medication that the doctor prescribes, including those for depression. If the doctor tells you to take the pill once a day with food, that is what you are agreeing to do every day unless otherwise instructed. If for some reason you cannot take a prescription medication, or you decide that you will not, you should tell your health-care practitioner as soon as possible so that they are up-to-date on the medications that you are taking and can suggest alternatives.

Over the years, however, we have found that many people, young and old alike, take their medications in a variety of creative ways that do not even resemble the medical instructions they were given. Sometimes it is done deliberately, but many people are unaware that what they are doing is incorrect, or that it could interfere in the drug's usefulness.

When you receive a prescription drug, the instructions for the dose that you should take and when to take it are based on research findings and your doctor's clinical experience. Drug manufacturers often spend many years determining what amount is most effective for treating a particular illness. At the same time, they determine what amount is unsafe for you to use. Unless your doctor tells you otherwise, you should always take the medication exactly as directed on the label. Of course, if serious side effects develop, you should immediately stop taking the medicine and call your doctor.

Avoid These Major Pitfalls!

As you are reading this, you may wonder if the way you take your medications is having a negative impact on their effectiveness. The following are some examples of dangerous pitfalls to avoid. See if you recognize yourself in any of these examples:

- **"I don't like taking any pills, not even an aspirin."** You may agree to take an antidepressant at the doctor's office and may even fill the prescription, but then leave it on the shelf. You may even tell the doctor that it didn't work. The doctor is under the impression that you have given this drug a fair trial when you have not.

- **"I'll take it, but only when I really need it."** You fill the prescription, but decide to wait until you feel more depressed to take it. On the really bad days, you take it but it doesn't seem to help. In fact, it upsets your stomach. You only take it three days in a row, but when you see your doctor the next month you tell her it's not working. She assumes that you have been taking it every day and decides that it must not be working, so she writes you a prescription for something else.

- **"I'm very sensitive to medications. I've had bad things happen to me after taking pills before. They scare me. I just know that I will be the one to have a bad reaction."** You relate your fears to the doctor but she encourages you to take the medication anyway. After taking one pill, you feel very anxious, dizzy, and sick to your stomach. You call your doctor's office in distress and refuse to take another of those pills. While it is possible that you are having a reaction to the drug, you could be experiencing some anxiety about taking it.

- **"If one is good for me, three will be better."** You hear the doctor tell you that it may take a month or two for the antidepressant to help you feel better. You decide that it would help to take a little bit more each day so that it will start to work faster. You have an increase in side effects and don't notice feeling any better. You tell your doctor that the pills did not work.

- **"It doesn't really matter if I miss a day or two, or what time I take it."** You may forget one day to take your antidepressant and decide that it did not make a big difference. You fall into a habit of taking it when you remember. After a while, you notice that the pill is not as effective and let your doctor know that you need something else. Your doctor assumes that you have been taking it as directed and gives you a different prescription.

- **"I'll take it, but I think that a quarter of a pill would be better for me than a whole one."** You know your body better than anyone else and you are sure that the medication is too strong for you. When your doctor tells you to start by taking one half of a pill and then increase to a whole in a few days, you decide that a quarter would be even better. Even though the pill is now in crumbs, you take a couple of the little pieces each day. After a few weeks, you report that you do not feel any better and that the medication is worthless.

A Common Sense Approach to Taking Drugs

Certainly you want to avoid doing things with medications that could at best be wasteful and at worst be a danger to your health. Here are a few tips for taking medications safely and to get the maximum benefit from them:

Take the right pill. Many people carry their pills with them when they go out, often putting them in other than their original containers. This is a good way to get confused about which pill is which and when you are supposed to take it. If you must take pills with you, it is preferable to keep them in their original container or in a secure medication box. Keep a list with you of the name of each pill, when you are supposed to take it, and what it looks like.

Take the right dose. Don't try to second-guess your doctor by deciding less or more is better. Swallowing tiny fragments of a pill will be about as effective as throwing the crumbs over your shoulder. Taking increased doses can be dangerous. You will not know whether something is really helpful or not if you are taking the wrong dose. If you feel strongly about the amount that you are taking, talk to your doctor. Together you may be able to come up with a solution that is right for you.

Take it at the right time. With your doctor's instruction, you may need to experiment initially with taking the pill at different times of day to determine which time will have the best effect on sleep and prevent daytime drowsiness. If you and your doctor decide that it is best for you to take your antidepressant at bedtime, stick with it. Try to take your pills within the same hour each day.

Take your medication and not someone else's. If you and your spouse keep your medication bottles side by side in the bathroom cabinet, be cautious about reaching for the wrong bottle. We have also encountered people who have held onto a deceased spouse's medication for years in the hopes of saving money. This is an unsafe practice. Dispose of medications that are not in use and not intended for you, and of your own medications after their expiration date has passed.

Let your doctor know of any changes in any other medications or new prescriptions prescribed to you by other health-care professionals. Generally speaking, the newer antidepressants are remarkably safe for use in combination with a variety of other medications. But interactions are possible. Your doctor and pharmacist will be the best judge of this possibility.

Let your doctor know of any nonprescription or over-the-counter drugs that you take regularly. This includes alternative medications, such as homeopathic and natural remedies. Again, interactions are possible and may be unsafe.

Do not drink alcohol when taking antidepressants. Alcohol is a central nervous system depressant. As you age, alcohol can have a greater impact on your mental functioning, even when consumed in smaller amounts. If you are going to make the effort to take an antidepressant, then you should do everything you can to maximize the desired effect.

Look at your caffeine intake. If you are having problems with anxiety, sleeplessness, or restlessness, caffeine can make you feel worse. Optimize the effect of the antidepressant that you are taking by reducing or eliminating your caffeine intake. Do this slowly over a few days or a week. Going cold turkey from caffeine can result in a major headache and other withdrawal symptoms.

If you have had repeated problems remembering to take your medications or get confused about whether you have actually taken them, you should talk frankly about this with your doctor. We have met many well-meaning, intelligent people who are unable to take their medications accurately. This can be particularly dangerous if you are uncertain if you have taken them and then take one more pill just to make sure. Poor management of medications can result in overdosing or underdosing. Warning signs of this type of drug misuse are running out of pills before the prescription indicates that you should, intermittent periods of confusion, or an unusual degree of side effects. See the goals at the end of the chapter for suggestions to remedy this risky habit.

"I've Tried Them All and None of Them Work"

We sometimes hear from an older adult that they have tried every antidepressant on the market and that all of them have failed to help relieve their symptoms. Others have told us that they have used a particular antidepressant and have been greatly helped by it for a couple of years—and then it loses its effectiveness. There are variations in response to medications.

If you are concerned that you have tried many different antidepressants and that they have failed, there are some possible solutions. After reading the material in this chapter, you may wonder if you actually stayed on a particular antidepressant long enough to give it a fair trial. You may have been discouraged by the initial side effects without realizing that they are usually temporary. You may have only been on the medication for a couple of days and expected it to work in that time. Remember that it may take many weeks to take effect and have an impact on your symptoms. Or you may have tried it years ago, before doctors understood the need to start the dose "low and go slow." If you suspect that any of these is true, ask your doctor to try that antidepressant again. Or there may be a newer drug that will help you.

Another possibility is that an antidepressant worked for a while and then seemed to lose its "oomph." Talk with your doctor about the dose. Some prescribing health-care professionals hear the advice "start low and go slow" and stop at the low starting dose. It is also possible that your antidepressant might work better if another antidepressant is added. This can often be done safely with good results. Again, consult your doctor or psychiatrist.

Many people get their psychiatric medications from their regular doctor. You may be asking your family practice doctor or primary care provider to address an issue that is not in their area of expertise. While some general practitioners and internists are quite knowledgeable about mental health issues and treatments, many have so many other types of medications and treatments to consider for your overall health that they may not be fully up-to-date about psychiatric medications. You can benefit from going to a psychiatrist or psychiatric nurse practitioner. They are specialists in the area of mental health who will be more informed about newer treatment options and better equipped to find the right medication for you.

If the depression you are experiencing has been difficult to treat or more complicated, you may need more aggressive treatment. Many older adults with severe depression who do not respond to medication or therapy do respond to another form of treatment, electroconvulsive therapy (ECT). This is particularly true if you have experienced psychotic symptoms (hearing voices or seeing things that other people can't hear or see, feeling paranoid or unusually suspicious of other people, having delusions) in addition to depression. Unlike the horrifying scenes in the movie *One Flew Over the Cuckoo's Nest*, ECT as performed today is a fairly safe and simple procedure. For very specific cases, ECT has been found to be very helpful for older adults with persistent forms of depression. As with any medical treatment, you should discuss with your doctor any risks or side effects before making a decision about this form of treatment.

Managing Costs

Regardless of how the debate turns out in terms of Medicare's role in paying for prescription drug costs, there are some things that you can do now to minimize your direct, out-of-pocket expenses for these costly medications. Most of the pharmaceutical manufacturers have "patient assistance" programs that will help people at certain income levels to obtain their prescribed medication at a reduced cost. The income requirements may vary from company to company, but it is worth finding out if you are eligible for such assistance. They also vary on the amount of assistance they will give you. For example, some will help you for a ninety-day period, while others may help for longer. Some require that your doctor contact them directly and others allow some other patient advocate—such as a nurse, pharmacist, or social worker—to verify your need. They generally will want to know your income, your insurance, and the prescription name and dose. They usually require your doctor to complete a form and provide a signature. The assistance will probably take a number of weeks or a month to process.

In the Resources section, you'll find a list of manufacturers, the antidepressant medication that they make, and the phone number to call to get information about their patient assistance program. Your doctor may already be aware of such a program, but do not hesitate to bring this up with them if they are not. Some companies will ask to deal directly with your physician, in which case you can give contacting information to your doctor's office. This list of antidepressants and the corresponding patient assistance program is devised from a list available on the National Alliance for the Mentally Ill Web site. You may go there for direct links to patient assistance information on the Web. (See Resources.) Further information about specific patient assistance programs can be found on the Pharmaceutical Research and Manufacturers of America Web site. (See Resources.) There is additional information from other sites and programs such as the Medicine Program, which helps you obtain all the applications for the drugs that you use. They are also listed in the Resources section of the book.

The following are some additional suggestions for reducing the costs that you incur for medications.

- When you first start a medication, ask your doctor for samples. Many doctors have these available for your initial use of the medication.

- If samples are not available, ask your pharmacist to fill only a portion of your prescription, say a couple of weeks' worth. You may have to pay more per pill than if you buy the larger quantity, but if you have an adverse reaction to a pill, and need to stop it, you will save money by having purchased only the smaller amount. If you tolerate the medications, the pharmacist can then fill the remainder of your prescription for you later.

- Sometimes the larger dose of a pill is a better bargain, and your doctor may be able to order a larger dose that you can cut in half. For example, if you are taking 50 mg of Zoloft once a day, you could purchase thirty 50 mg tablets of Zoloft for $79.21 to last you one month. But thirty of the 100 mg tablets of Zoloft cost only $80.99. You could cut these in half and pay literally half as much for a month's supply! Remember, we are not suggesting that you chop up pills into tiny parts and guess how much to take. But many pills have a "score" in the middle that allows them to be broken or cut in half easily. Talk to your doctor and your pharmacist about this potentially huge money-saver.

- Ask your pharmacist about the most cost-effective form of the drug you are taking. Unfortunately, most of the newer drugs are not available in generic form, though this will change in the next several years. Prozac, as the oldest of the SSRIs, will be running out of its patent and should be available as a generic by July 2001. There may be a difference in cost in the form of the medication from tablets to liquids to capsules. For instance, Remeron is available in a chewable tablet formulation that costs less than the traditional tablet form of the same dose.

Fay's Story

Fay is a seventy-nine-year-old woman who has suffered many hardships. Following a bypass operation two years ago, she not only became depressed but also had a fall in her bathroom that resulted in a broken hip. "I was so tired of being in the hospital. I just wanted to go home and be back in my own world." But after hip replacement surgery and going back home, Fay had more problems. She had an adverse reaction to the pain medication that she was taking for her hip. She became confused and even hallucinated. She could not sleep at night and called out constantly to her daughter, with whom she lived.

Finally, her daughter took her back to the hospital, where Fay was admitted to the psychiatric unit. The doctors treated her for her depression as well as delirium that had developed from her pain medications. The doctors were able to treat her with several medications. They changed her antidepressant to a new one and added an antipsychotic medication to help decrease her unclear thinking and hallucinations. Fay was able to sleep again. She began to feel more like her old self after her frightening experience. She was discharged from the hospital to home.

But on a follow-up visit with the psychiatrist a few weeks later, Fay seemed worse. She was having difficulty sleeping again and was terrified when her daughter was out of her sight. She was confused at times. After discussing her symptoms in detail with the doctor, Fay could not understand why she was feeling so distressed again. The doctor called Fay's daughter to get more information. In the conversation, Fay's daughter mentioned that they had not been able to buy the new medications when Fay was discharged from the hospital because they were so expensive. She would have had to choose between buying the new psychiatric pills and medications for Fay's blood pressure and heart. Her daughter had been giving Fay the old pills that Fay had been taking before she went to the hospital. Fay was unaware of this, as she had relied on her daughter to give her the right pills.

The doctor was able to give Fay samples of the new medications, and his office filled out the paperwork to get patient assistance from the drug companies for her. "After a few weeks, I started to get better again. It was a real lesson for me and my daughter. I still don't know how we are going to manage these bills. But I'm better off taking care of it now than I was without the right pills."

Goal 23: Know Your Medications

Write down which pill you are taking or considering and what it is supposed to treat. Write down all the other drugs you are taking also, and what their purposes are. Talk about this with your coach and with your doctor the next time you have an appointment. Make sure to clarify any questions that you may have about each medication with your doctor or pharmacist.

Medication	**Reason I Take It**

Goal 24: Make Your Doctor Your Personal Expert

Throughout this chapter, we have suggested questions that you should discuss with your doctor to have the best understanding and information about your medications and health. Many people think of questions that they want to know about after they leave the doctor's office or forget to ask the ones they have thought about before they went. You have a right to the information pertaining to your health. You can make the most of your and your doctor's time together by being prepared and having your questions written down. Here are a few suggested questions that you can take with you to your doctor's office:

- What are the expected side effects of the medication that I am taking? How long should I expect to have these side effects?

- What should I do if I miss a dose?

- What is the dose that I will need to take to get the maximum benefit?

- Will I be able to reduce the dose at a later time?

- How long will I need to take this medication?

- What should I do if I decide that I want to stop taking this drug?

- How does this drug interact with the medications that I am already taking?

- What is the best time of day for me to take this medication? Should I take it with food?

Now write down any further questions that you may have for your doctor about your medications:

1. _____

2. _____

3. _____

Goal 25: Clean Out Your Medicine Cabinet!

Do you have old bottles of pills stacked in the medicine cabinet? We meet lots of older adults who hang on to bags full of pill bottles in the hopes that they will be able to use them at some point in the future. There are many problems with this practice: medications lose their effectiveness over time, your doctor may not want you to combine an older drug with a newer one, or you may forget the original purpose of the drug and take it for incorrect reasons. Most pharmacists advise that medicines be thrown out after one year from the date of purchase if you have not used them. Look through your medicine cabinet or other places that you store your pills and discard the expired medications.

Review of medications and disposal of expired ones was completed on: _____

Goal 26: Refine Your System

What's your system for taking pills and making sure that you have taken them accurately every day? Being consistent is the key. Here are some ideas to help you take your pills accurately every day:

- If you keep your pill bottles in the kitchen, don't move them to another place to be forgotten. Keep them somewhere where you will see them every day, serving as a visual reminder to take them.

- Avoid keeping medications by your bedside. You may get confused in the night and take additional doses. Remember, taking medication requires your attention and care. You should not be fumbling with medication bottles when you are half asleep.

- One woman we know used the following method to keep her pills straight: She kept her pills in their original containers. She lined up her bottles on a specific shelf in her kitchen cabinet. When she took her medication during the day, she would turn the bottle upside down to remind her that she had indeed taken her pill. If she had to take an additional dose of the same pill later in the day, she would move that bottle to a second shelf. At the end of the day, she would turn the bottles right side up and return them to the first shelf before going to bed. She could always look at her shelves during the day and tell whether she had taken the last dose. This method would work best if you have a small number of pills to take each day.

- Many people like to use a plastic medication box to sort their pills by dose and time of day. There are many varieties available at your pharmacy. If possible, practice opening the compartments of the box before purchasing, because some can be very difficult to open if you have problems such as arthritis. If you have had problems with taking the right pills at the right time, this can be very helpful. The key is to put the correct pills in the pill box.

- If you have had frequent problems with forgetting to take pills, we advise that you have someone else present when you fill your pill box each week to double check your accuracy or even fill your pill box for you. A member of your family, a friend, or your coach could call you to remind you to take pills at certain times. Some emergency response services for older adults will also provide this type of call. It is important for you to confront this problem honestly. You may hesitate to get help with this because of concern about limiting your independence. But by getting some assistance with your medications, you may be decreasing the risk of confusion or falls; proper medication will help you preserve your independence, not threaten it.

- You can use a medication checklist to monitor your accuracy and consistency in taking your medications. A sample medication checklist is shown below. To use it, simply place a check in the appropriate box after taking each pill.

Monday	Tuesday	Wednesday	Thursday	Friday	Saturday	Sunday
Morning: Aspirin	*Morning*: Aspirin	*Morning*: Aspirin	*Morning*: Aspirin	*Morning*: Aspirin	*Morning*: Aspirin	*Morning*: Aspirin
Vasotec	Vasotec	Vasotec	Vasotec	Vasotec	Vasotec	Vasotec
Zoloft	Zoloft	Zoloft	Zoloft	Zoloft	Zoloft	Zoloft
Evening: Trazodone	*Evening*: Trazodone	*Evening*: Trazodone	*Evening*: Trazodone	*Evening*: Trazodone	*Evening*: Trazodone	*Evening*: Trazodone

Which of these suggestions sounds right for you to improve your system of taking medications?

_____

_____

Below is an outline of a medication checklist for you to fill out with your own medications. Don't forget to include all of your medications.

Monday	Tuesday	Wednesday	Thursday	Friday	Saturday	Sunday
Morning:	_Morning:_	_Morning:_	_Morning:_	_Morning:_	_Morning:_	_Morning:_
Afternoon:	_Afternoon:_	_Afternoon:_	_Afternoon:_	_Afternoon:_	_Afternoon:_	_Afternoon:_
Evening:	_Evening:_	_Evening:_	_Evening:_	_Evening:_	_Evening:_	_Evening:_

Making the choice to take medications for depression can be difficult. When you do decide to take any medication, taking an active, responsible role in how you take it can improve your chances of a positive outcome.

Chapter 7

Anxiety: You Can Gain Control

Many people experience anxiety along with depression. In this chapter you will learn the difference between the two and how to focus on simple, even enjoyable goals and exercises that will help you to feel in control again.

Vern's Story

Vern is a tall and slender eighty-two-year-old man with a slight stoop to his posture. He has always prided himself on his athletic nature and abilities. He plays in a senior softball league each year and swims daily at the local YMCA. When Vern was in his fifties, he and his wife divorced. "We had come to a mutual agreement that it was over between us. Our children were grown, and though it was hard for them to understand at first, they have adjusted. I still meet periodically with my ex for lunch or coffee, and I consider her a trusted friend."

Several years ago, Vern met a lovely woman named Jean who had moved a couple of doors down from his condo. They had a whirlwind romance and married three months later. After Jean and Vern went on a cruise to the Caribbean, Vern developed pneumonia. He was in the hospital for several days and then returned home. "They told me that I was fine, but I didn't feel fine. I'm the kind of guy who never gets sick and this pneumonia really took it out of me. I just didn't feel quite right after that."

In spite of Jean's encouragement to get back into his usual activities, Vern found that he was feeling depressed much of the time. Then the worrying began. Vern describes it this way: "I started worrying more about my health. I've always taken such good care of my health and I've been so physically active. I kept asking myself over and over, why is this happening to me?" He began to worry about every decision that he'd made, especially that he had married Jean. "I started to wonder what I had done to her life, now that I was becoming so ill. I was sure that I would die soon. I felt terribly guilty." After a while, Vern found that he was worrying about almost everything.

At first, Vern would try to get himself to think about other things. But the fears and worry would creep into his thoughts even when he was trying to do something else, like read a book. He felt keyed up and would pace in the living room, unable to sit down for any period of time. His muscles ached with tension. At night, he would lie awake going over and over his worried thoughts. He felt tired all day long.

Finally, Jean insisted that they go to Vern's doctor together. The doctor did a complete examination. "The doctor informed me that I had depression and anxiety. She was very matter of fact about it, but she let me know that I needed to do something about it." The doctor recommended an antidepressant and a therapist. "I was very skeptical. I really didn't believe that there were any solutions for what was happening to me and that people just didn't understand how bad off I was. But slowly, I started to feel a little bit better. Then I started to put more effort into it. It took some time, but I feel much better. Now, I still have to be careful and watch out for that worrying. When I notice that I am worrying more, I do some of the things that I learned about decreasing stress from the therapist. I'm back to swimming every day. Jean and I are planning a trip out West. I'm so grateful that I am living my life again, instead of worrying about it."

Depression and Anxiety, Hand In Hand

Depression and anxiety are both normal responses to certain life events. But when either becomes excessive or long-lasting, it causes great emotional pain. While experiencing a clinical depression is bad enough, many people also have some degree of anxiety along with it. There is no definitive explanation as to why people with depression often have anxiety too. Both are clearly impacted by physical and emotional stress, which influences brain functioning and chemistry.

Anxiety can be described as a sense of unease or apprehension. This feeling is sometimes a vague undercurrent that accompanies distressing and intrusive thoughts about bad things that you fear will happen. When people are anxious, they experience a variety of feelings and changes in their bodies, both physical and emotional.

Exercise: Sorting Through Your Feelings

Here are some ways other people describe their anxiety. As you read through the lists, place a check by the descriptions that match your experience.

Check	Physical Cues	Check	Emotional Cues
	Feeling tense or edgy		"A case of nerves"
	"Butterflies in my stomach"		Feeling more sensitive than usual
	Racing heart		Frequent worrying
	Sweaty palms		"I can't think straight"
	Dry mouth		Easily annoyed or irritable
	Restlessness, can't sit still		Fearful or afraid
	Fidgety		Panic
	Dizziness		Apprehension
	Nausea		Distress
	Frequent diarrhea		Nervous

Many people tell us that they are aware of feeling "more depressed than anxious" or "more anxious than depressed." If you are aware of having some anxiety, are you aware of whether it has a stronger presence than the depressed mood? Write down your thoughts about that here:

_____

_____

_____

_____

Different Types of Anxiety

There are a number of different types of anxiety. We will describe a few of the more common types and provide a checklist for each, based on the criteria of the *Diagnostic and Statistical Manual of Mental Disorders, Fourth Edition* (DSM-IV-TR). The types of anxiety described below are Generalized Anxiety Disorder, Panic Attack, Obsessive-Compulsive Disorder, and Post-Traumatic Stress Disorder. Check those that apply to you and discuss the features that you check with your doctor, a psychiatrist, or a therapist. Having some of the features listed does not necessarily mean that you have the diagnosis, but may indicate that there is a problem that needs to be addressed. Remember, because of the physical features of anxiety, you should have a complete physical by your doctor to rule out any medical conditions. Only a trained professional can make the diagnosis of anxiety.

Generalized Anxiety Disorder

- You feel anxious or worried more days than not for at least six months. You worry about common events, such as everyday activities or your family.

- You find that once you start to worry, it is hard to control it.

- You feel restless or keyed up.

- You are easily tired.

- You have poor concentration.

- You are more irritable than is normal for you.

- You have muscle tension, such as in your neck, jaw, or hands.

- You have problems falling or staying asleep, or restless sleep.

Example of Generalized Anxiety Disorder

"I've always been a worrier, but lately I feel like my thoughts are out of control. I worry about every little thing, all day long, and just feel exhausted by the end of the day. But then, when I finally crawl into bed, my mind just won't shut off. I can't get to sleep until 2 or 3 A.M."

Panic Attack

Panic attacks can occur spontaneously; there may be one episode or many. In any event, they are frightening experiences for those who have them.

- You may have a sudden and intense rush of fear or discomfort, reaching a peak in about ten minutes.

- Your heart is pounding or beating fast.

- You're sweating.

- You feel shaky or your hands tremble.

- You feel short of breath.

- You feel like you are choking.

- You have chest pain or discomfort.

- You feel nauseated or have other stomach distress.

- You are dizzy or light-headed.

- You feel disconnected or unreal.

- You feel like you are going crazy or like you will lose control.

- You are afraid that you could die.

- You feel numbness or tingling.

- You feel chilled or hot.

An Example of a Panic Attack

"It just hits me right out the blue. I feel like I'm going to go crazy. I've gone to the emergency room a couple of times thinking that I am having a heart attack, but then they tell me that my heart is fine and I am having a panic attack. I'm terribly afraid that it will happen again."

Obsessive-Compulsive Disorder

Obsessions are repetitive, intrusive, and distressing thoughts or images. Compulsions are rituals or other behaviors that you do to try to prevent or decrease a feeling of anxiety or the obsessive thought. You may or may not realize over time that the thoughts or behavior are unreasonable. Many people experience these in milder forms but when they become time-consuming and interfere with your ability to do other things, the condition may warrant treatment. Use the following checklists to determine if you should discuss this further with a mental health professional:

Obsessions:

- You have disturbing thoughts that intrude on your other thoughts.

- These thoughts are more than excessive worry about everyday problems, and you realize that the thoughts are only in your mind.

- You attempt to push these thoughts away.

Compulsions:

- You engage in repetitive activities such as excessive hand washing or checking the locks, or mental activity such as repeating words over and over or counting.

- The action is compelled by your need to get rid of an obsessive thought.

- You perform the behavior to reduce a feeling of tension or anxiety.

An Example of an Obsession

"I can't stop worrying about my granddaughter. I can be doing something else, like buying groceries. Thoughts of my granddaughter being attacked or getting into a car accident just pop into my head. It's horrible. I think about all the terrible details and I can't seem to stop myself. I think about this over and over every day. Sometimes, I think, if I have these thoughts, it might prevent it from happening to her. I keep trying to tell myself that there is no reason for me to think that these things will happen to her, but it doesn't work."

An Example of a Compulsion

"My wife always called me a packrat, but it seems like in the last few years, it's gotten much worse. I've collected so many books and magazines that I haven't had a chance to read. I can hardly move around my condo, and I can't find anything that I need. I know that it sounds strange, but I just can't seem to let go of this stuff. I should give the magazines away or donate the books to the library but I cannot seem to make myself do it. It upsets me to think that I might miss out on something important if I don't read them."

Post-Traumatic Stress Disorder

You might think of Post-Traumatic Stress Disorder (PTSD) as the condition that develops following a wartime trauma. It was often referred to in the past as "battle fatigue" or being "shell-shocked." However, PTSD can be the result of any traumatic event, such as a natural disaster (a hurricane or a tornado), a serious car accident, or a violent attack. Check the following symptoms and review them with a professional if indicated:

- You have experienced an event that involved the actual or threatened death or serious injury of yourself or others. Your response to this event includes enormous fear, helplessness, or horror.

- You have recurrent thoughts and memories that cause distress.

- You have recurring dreams related to the event.

- You feel that the event is still happening.

- You experience extreme distress when you are reminded of the event by things around you.

- You notice feelings of numbness regarding your present life and avoid anything that reminds you of the event.

- You are easily aroused or startled in a way that did not affect you prior to the event. You may have sleep problems or extreme irritability or angry outbursts, or be overly watchful of things happening around you.

Examples of PTSD

1. "I was an infantryman in World War II. I always thought that I had dealt with what I saw over there pretty well. About a year ago, my wife died suddenly. Sometime after that, I started to have dreams about the war. Terrible nightmares. If I saw anything on television about fighting anywhere in the world, I would know that I would have more dreams that night. I had to stop watching the news. I would be sitting in my chair and jump if I heard a loud sound outside. I couldn't think straight."

2. "I was always afraid of water as a young girl and I never learned how to swim. My husband and I retired to a beautiful place out in the country. A couple of years ago, there were torrential rains and without any warning, there were flash floods. My husband had gone into town and I was alone without a car. The water kept rising and before I really understood what was happening, water was pouring into the house. I tried to run, but the

water knocked me down and carried me outside. Somehow, I managed to hang onto a tree and that's where they found me hours later.

"Now, my husband and I are both fine physically, but I keep seeing that water rising and pulling me away in my mind. I have had so many nightmares that I am afraid to go to sleep at night. I haven't been able to go back out to our place. I don't even want to talk about it. I hate to admit it, but I'm even afraid of the water in the bathtub, and I avoid getting in. I feel like my life is over, that a part of me got taken away by that flood."

Exercise: Rating Your Own Anxiety

After reading about the different types of anxiety, you probably have a better idea if anxiety is a problem for you. You can learn about your level of anxiety by rating it on a scale of 1 to 10, with 1 signifying a small amount of unease, but feeling relatively calm. At the other end of the scale, a 10 would mean that you feel very anxious, like climbing the walls. Rate the level of anxiety that you feel now:

---

1   2   3   4   5   6   7   8   9   10

Because anxiety is so often expressed in a physical way, it can also be helpful for you to monitor your level of physical tension. Use the same scale of 1 to 10. Think of 1 to represent feeling that your muscles are warm, relaxed, and loose. At the other end of the scale, a 10 means that your muscles are very tight, clenched, and sore. What is the number that you would assign to the feeling of physical tension that you have right now?

---

1   2   3   4   5   6   7   8   9   10

Another feature of anxiety is your energy level. With anxiety, you may feel much nervous energy at first, but over time, you can feel both fatigue and restlessness. Again, we will use a scale of 1 to 10. 1 equals a feeling of low energy. 10 indicates a high level of energy or restlessness that is difficult to contain. Rate your feeling of energy now:

1   2   3   4   5   6   7   8   9   10

Perhaps there are certain times of day or certain occasions that cause you to feel particularly anxious. Discuss these with your coach. Share this information about how you have rated your anxiety. Also discuss what these numbers mean for you.

What Is Stress?

Stress is a natural and unavoidable fact of life. Stress occurs whenever you are faced with situations that you cannot easily manage or that require you to change. Good events and bad events can cause stress. Growing older has its own unique stressors. Regardless of the source, excessive stress can lead to anxiety and depression.

It helps to start by thinking of how your body and your mind react to stress. When you are facing a stressful situation, hormones (also referred to as neurochemicals) are released in your body. In particular, adrenaline and cortisol are released into the bloodstream from the adrenal glands, located above the kidneys.

These hormones play a role in initiating the well-known "fight or flight" response: blood vessels constrict, causing your blood pressure to soar and blood to flow to the large muscles of your body, such as to your legs, to increase your ability to run or fight. This response is very helpful for emergency situations. The stress response helps push you into action so that you can survive physically threatening situations, such as if a there were a fire in your house and you needed to get out. These physical responses are accompanied by feelings of restlessness, agitation, and nervousness; you feel your stomach churn, your hands feel clammy, your muscles tighten. Normally, only small amounts of neurochemicals are released when the stressors are small. But in our complicated and stressful lives, your body may become conditioned to initiate the stress response more frequently. Some people are found to release large amounts of these hormones, even when faced with small daily stressors. Over time, large amounts of cortisol in the system can compromise the immune response, impairing your body's ability to fight off disease. The level of stress in your life impacts how your body responds to many medical conditions, such as heart disease, irritable bowel syndrome, and high blood pressure. In other words, reducing stress is a critical component of emotional and physical health. We will talk about specific ways to reduce stress later in the chapter.

Special Issues That You Face as You Get Older

As an older adult, you face a number of unique stressors. Many younger people are unaware of the frequency and intensity of stressors that older people encounter in their daily life. Not all stressors are negative situations. Even some good things that happen to you can cause stress if they require a big change in your life. We can look at these stressors as either environmental or emotional. How you adapt or respond to the stressors of life is the key to how much the particular stress will impact you.

Environmental Stress

You may not even realize that aspects of your environment are a source of stress. Long-held patterns may contribute to stress, but so may sudden changes. And even things you think of as small irritations can add considerably to your stress level.

Typical examples of environmental stressors are:

- **The condition of the home you live in:** Over the years, has your home become too large for your needs? Is it difficult for you to maintain? Is your home filled with clutter that you cannot seem to part with? Is it accessible, or do you have difficulty getting upstairs to your bedroom or into the basement to wash clothes? Is your neighborhood safe or are you at risk? Have you moved recently?

- **Your daily routine:** Are you able to eat nutritious foods in adequate amounts each day? Are you able to bathe, dress, and maintain daily chores in your home?

- **Your finances:** Do you have enough money to buy medications that you need? Do you worry that you will not be able to make ends meet now or in the future?

- **Your health:** Is your health changing? Are you able to walk easily or with assistive devices? Do you have chronic pain? Is it difficult for you to go places because of your health? Are you in pain on a daily basis? Do you have a chronic or a terminal illness?

- **Your mode of transportation:** Do you drive or take a bus? Do you rely on other people to give you rides?

Goal 27: Find the Stress Culprit!

Identify the environmental stressors listed above that you relate to. Discuss what you write down with your coach. Then do some brainstorming about possible ways to decrease these environmental stressors such as hooking up with social services in your community, taking a more proactive stance with your health care, or looking at housing options. Be sure to write down your possible solutions.

Emotional Stress

Emotional stressors can affect you at any age. As when you were younger, you may notice that you are able to handle some changes and stressors more easily than others. But when you are depressed or become anxious, you may notice that your tolerance for such stress is diminished. Some people describe this as having a stress limit. Once you have gone over the limit of the stress that you can manage, it seems that everything causes you stress.

Some examples of emotional stressors are:

- **The amount of support that you have from other people in your life:** Do you have people you can count on to help you in everyday situations and emergencies? Do you talk to people close to you every day or only on occasion?

- **Loss of loved ones:** Have you recently lost someone you have been close to? Has a good friend or trusted family member moved far away? Have you moved away from people you have known for a long time? Have you or someone in your family been through a divorce that has altered a relationship with someone else in your family?

- **Family changes:** Are you a caretaker for a spouse or other member of your family? Have there been new additions to your family? Have you become a grandparent or a great-grandparent? Has one of your children recently remarried, bringing new step-grandchildren into your life? Have you gotten involved in family conflicts? Have people in your family had to deal with stressful changes such as illness, loss of job, or loss of home that have in turn impacted you?

Goal 28: Your Emotional Triggers to Stress

Identify and write down the emotional stressors that have impacted your life. Talk with your coach about the most important of them.

_____

_____

_____

_____

Stress in Relationships

Of all the issues that cause stress, conflict in relationships is what we hear the most about. Very often, this involves some concern, disagreement, or imbalance in a relationship with an older adult and their grown children or grandchildren. Older adults express great concern and puzzlement about the difference in the lifestyles of their offspring compared to their own. Consider the numbers of dual-income families, how many children are in day care with non-family caretakers, the increased rate of divorce, remarriage, cohabitation, drug abuse, layoffs, and the technology boom and all its implications on daily life. The modern life lived by many younger people today can seem chaotic, fast-paced, and overwhelming to a generation that had a simpler way of living. Many older adults feel stress and worry greatly about how their families will handle their own level of stress.

It is a natural tendency to want to help your family deal with their life difficulties. There are many positive outcomes related to stepping in and providing needed support. Family cohesion can be strengthened and problem solving can be enhanced. But for some people, "helping out" can blur the meaning of independence and dependence for both parents and adult children. In order for children to become responsible adults, they need to experience their own successes and failures, to learn from mistakes and discover ways to solve problems. While your desire to help your child and protect him never stops, it can be harmful to take too much responsibility away from an adult child. Every time you take care of something that an adult should be handling on their own, you take away an opportunity for them to learn from their experience and grow. It can create dependence and resentment toward you for limiting their control of their own life. You also may become resentful of being the only responsible adult.

One way to clarify your responsibilities and your children's responsibilities is to talk about them together. This is referred to as setting limits. Clear communication is critical in relationships to define what you need or expect from others, rather than letting assumptions, and thus confusion, rule. Setting limits helps everyone to understand what is expected of them and to know what they are accountable for in their lives.

Harriet's Story

Harriet, a seventy-six-year-old native of Minnesota, has always been known for her sense of humor and her kind and generous nature. Harriet raised her granddaughter, Rebecca. Rebecca was the source of Harriet's worry and stress. As a teenager, Rebecca got involved with drugs. Rebecca made it through high school, and moved out on her own, but became more involved with drugs. At twenty-three, she had a baby. Harriet urged her to move back in with her. Harriet took Rebecca to a drug treatment program and paid for most of it out of her savings. Harriet retired from her job and stayed home to take care of Rebecca and the baby. Since then, Rebecca had managed to stay away from drugs, but could not seem to hold down a job. She watched television much of the day and yelled at Harriet to get off her case. "At the time, I thought that Rebecca was trying as much as she could. I hardly had any savings left. I really didn't know what we were going to do. I couldn't afford to keep paying for all of us to live here. But what would happen to the baby if I asked Rebecca to move out? I was so depressed and worried all the time. My blood pressure started to get much worse. My doctor told me that I had to cut out stress, but all I could think was, how do I do that?"

Harriet's doctor told her about a therapy group for people with depression. "When I started going to the group and told them about my problems, I thought that they really didn't understand. They kept asking me to talk about myself, and not Rebecca. I began to realize that I had forgotten about what I really wanted in life because I have been so consumed by Rebecca's problems."

Harriet began to learn about how she had taken over all the responsibilities for each person in the household. The group had Harriet practice how she could ask for what she needed from Rebecca and start to set some limits. "It turned out she was very unhappy too. We began to make some plans together. We set a time limit for when Rebecca would move out of the house. It gave her enough time to start a job and save a little money. It's been hard for her, but she has done it. Rebecca enrolled her child in a preschool. Now I have a little freedom. Things aren't perfect, but we've been getting along better. I am trying to stop solving all of Rebecca's problems and pay more attention to my own. I'm bowling more and I'm seeing more of my friends."

Exercise: Strive for Balance

When you consider your relationships with family and other loved ones, do you wonder if you have made your limits clear or fuzzy? Does your lack of clear limits affect your stress and anxiety levels? Remember, it can be healthy to help others as long as there is a balance between give and take. But without that balance, you bear an unfair burden. Here are some questions to ask yourself. Write the answers down and discuss them with your coach or your therapist.

1. Do you feel responsible for the problems of other people in your family or in your life?

_____

_____

2. Do you feel guilty if you don't do things for your children or others, even if doing so places a hardship on you?

_____

_____

3. Do you wish that you could say "no" but always say "yes"?

_____

_____

4. Do you believe that the needs of other people are more important than your needs?

_____

_____

5. Do you resent the effort that you put forth and feel continually disappointed in others?

_____

_____

An answer of "yes" to any of the above questions indicates that your limit setting may need some adjusting. A good way to clarify your boundaries and decrease your stress level is to understand what your own needs are. We each have needs from ourselves and from other people. Write down what some of your needs are, being as specific as possible. For example, instead of saying "I need love from my children," try "I need to hear from my children once a week." Also, consider what you need and expect from yourself, such as "I will be responsible for saying what I really think instead of keeping it to myself."

What I need from myself:

_____

_____

_____

What I need from the people that I love:

_____

_____

_____

It does little good to understand your needs if you do not communicate them to the people who should hear them. Don't fall into the trap of thinking, "They should already know what I need." Do not expect people to read your mind. This assumption will only lead to resentment on your part. Practice saying your needs out loud to your coach, and then try it on the people who you want to know your needs. Practicing clear communication and limit setting is essential for you to decrease your stress and anxiety level. Say what you need every day.

Relaxation: The Key to Feeling in Control

Many people bristle at the term "relaxation." "I feel so anxious, how am I supposed to relax? It's impossible." Or you might be suspicious of what it means: Is it some mysterious secret mantra? Is it hypnotism? Do you fear that someone else will be able to control you?

Relaxation is actually a term to describe any activity that helps you decrease or manage feelings of tension, stress, or anxiety. This can include everyday activities as well as special exercises that you can easily learn. Perhaps you have used some form of relaxation or meditation in your life already. If you have found that your method of relaxation has become less effective recently, this may be a time to explore some new approaches. Many forms of relaxation are being used with good results to help people manage many other life problems and health issues such as to improve pain control, to heighten athletic and scholastic performance, and to ease the process of childbirth.

You may find it easier to think of relaxation as "anxiety management," or a way to gain a feeling of control. No matter what you call it, there are numerous ways for you to feel more at ease. Many people not only feel more in control, but also enjoy their relaxation time. The methods that we will describe are fairly straightforward and simple.

Each anxiety-management tool will take practice and repeated use, but they are generally easy to do and effective for decreasing feelings of anxiety. Keep in mind that every method does not work for everybody. While one technique can help you relax, it may do little to help another person. You may have to try several methods or combine methods before you find a regimen that works for you.

If you are taking antidepressants that also help with anxiety, you might wonder why you should bother with relaxation techniques. While medication is an important tool for managing depression and anxiety, it cannot be relied on solely to contain your response to everyday stress and tension. We have heard people suggest that whenever a stressful event occurs, "I can just take more of my medication." It would be great if you could simply increase your medications, like the volume control on the stereo, every time life got more challenging. But medication doesn't work that way, and taking greater doses than your doctor prescribes can be dangerous (see chapter 6). Stress and its impact are inherent in life, and it is essential that you arm yourself with additional coping skills that allow you to feel more in control. This is true regardless of whether you are taking medication or not.

Suggestions for Getting Started

1. Some people enjoy going to a relaxation class where there are other people and an instructor to guide you. Or you may prefer privacy. Some examples are:

- Relaxation and stress reduction classes held at senior centers

- Yoga, tai chi, or qigong classes offering the combined benefit of strength building and mental relaxation

- Excellent videos and tapes for relaxation that you can do in your own home (see some suggestions in the Resources section.)

2. When you practice in your home, set aside a space that will be exclusively for this activity. It should be quiet and as clear as possible. Just like having a desk to study at, you need a designated space for relaxation. Even if your space is restricted and you need to use your bedroom, you can enhance your experience by having simple things on hand that will awaken your senses. These can be special and meaningful cues that make it easier for you to get in the mood to relax. There are many options, including:

- lighting a scented candle

- spreading a deep-colored cloth or a beautiful scarf that you enjoy looking at over the bed or floor

- starting your practice with a hand massage using a scented lotion (see Goal 30); a simple clean scent, such as citrus or green apple, may be most effective

- playing quiet music or natural sounds of the ocean or a river

3. Give yourself time. You do not have to spend hours at a time doing relaxation exercises to feel better. Start with five to ten minutes, once or twice a day. Make it part of your daily routine. Consistency and regular repetition are key. Think about enjoying this time as a break from the other demands of your day.

4. If you feel very anxious, it can be hard to get started. Do some simple physical exercise prior to beginning your relaxation practice. Make it easy movement, such as five minutes of walking, chair or bed exercises and stretching, even dancing. This will help you feel more connected to your body, improve your circulation, and warm your body temperature.

5. Relaxation is about quieting your thoughts and clearing your mind. Turn the phone down. Turn the television off. Do not allow yourself to be interrupted.

Great! Now you are ready to begin some goals for relaxation and get back that feeling of control.

Goal 29: Practice Deep Breathing

It's free, it's easy, and you can do it anywhere, anytime! We have found that the practice of deep breathing is particularly useful in helping the older adults that we have worked with to feel better and think more clearly. It is fairly easy to master and requires only that you practice it regularly each day. As we get older, we tend to breathe less deeply. In addition, when you are nervous, you tend to breathe more quickly, with shallow breaths. This can result in less oxygen in your body. The effect of low oxygen on the brain can be confusion and sluggish thinking. The practice of deep breathing will help you to increase the oxygen in your body and your brain, decreasing the excitability of the nervous system and resulting in a sense of physical and mental calm.

Let's get started:

1. Concentrate on slow and deep breaths, both when you inhale and when you exhale.

2. Inhale through your nose and exhale blowing slowly and softly through your mouth.

3. Make your mouth into an "O" as you breathe out. Make a soft whooshing sound as the air leaves your body. Think about blowing out a candle very softly.

4. If you have any respiratory problems such as asthma or emphysema, take your time and do the breathing as is comfortable for you. It will be easier to start in a sitting or upright position.

5. Now, close your eyes and try deep breathing for about two minutes. Good! It's really pretty easy.

Here are some suggestions to improve your technique and get the most out of your deep breathing practice.

• Practice in different positions to become more aware of the feeling of breathing deeply. In a sitting position, sit up but be cautious of holding your shoulders too tightly; let them drop like loose noodles.

• Let your stomach expand as you inhale. When you practice lying on the floor or the bed, rest your hand on your abdomen and feel the rise and fall of your belly. The more deeply you breathe, the more you will notice this.

• You may practice standing up. Raise your arms as you breathe in and slowly lower them as you breathe out. This combination will not only help you relax but also wake you up and improve your energy.

- Visualize the air that you breathe in as cool and clean and watch it slowly flow into your lungs. Imagine the flow of the air all the way to your toes. Think of the air that leaves your body as tired and worn. Let this air move out of you like a slow leak from a tire with your mouth being the air valve. Let yourself make the sound of the slow leak with your mouth as you exhale. Let the air flow evenly.

- Imagine a big circle in front of you as you breathe. When you inhale, you travel from the bottom of the circle up one side slowly. You get to the top of the circle and, if you can, hold your breath for a few seconds. Then start to exhale slowly, traveling down the other side of the circle. The amount of time that it takes to travel up and down the sides of the circle is the same.

- A good way to measure how long you are practicing is to start with touching the tips of your thumb and first finger of one hand. Take your first deep breath and slowly exhale. Then touch the tips of your thumb with your second finger, and breathe deeply again. Repeat this sequence with each finger on each hand. When you finish both hands, you have finished practicing.

Practice deep breathing twice a day for at least two to five minutes every day this week when you are feeling fairly calm. When you feel yourself overcome by negative thoughts or anxiety, practice for at least five minutes. Write down what it feels like for you to do this and how it may be helping you. Talk with your coach and ask him or her to remind you to do your deep breathing or even practice with you.

Goal 30: Give Yourself a Hand Massage

Here's another simple and effective relaxation tool that you can do easily in your home. All you need is some hand or body lotion. Not only will you feel more relaxed, but it's great for your skin. Here's how:

- If you like, warm the lotion slightly for a more pleasant effect. Put a small amount of lotion (about 1½ tablespoons) in a small bowl and heat it in your microwave for a few seconds (ovens vary, so be careful not to overheat the lotion).

- Rub the lotion between both hands until you feel warmth.

- With one hand, rub a circle with your fingers into the other hand's palm for a moment or two.

- Grab that hand's thumb, twisting gently with the lotion and your fingers, moving from the base to the end of the thumb.

- Move to the space between your thumb and first finger. Gently pinch and rub the muscles in that space with your other hand's thumb and first finger.

- Then move to stroke each finger slowly as you started with your thumb and each space between each finger. Really pay attention to how good this feels and how it brings a feeling of warmth to your hand. When you finish one hand, do the same with the other.

- Take your time, breathe evenly as you do so, and enjoy!

Set a time to practice the hand massage. How did it feel? Is this a technique that you could practice once a week?

_____

_____

Goal 31: Try a Unique and Calming Face Massage

We have practiced this technique with older adults and it has been very popular. It is loosely based on a traditional Chinese practice. This is simple and easy to do at home or anywhere that you need to unwind. After doing this quick exercise, we often hear people say, "Ahhhh!" Here's how to do it:

- Take off your glasses or jewelry such as earrings or necklaces. If you wear hearing aids, you may want to turn them off or remove them.

- Rub your hands together lightly, feeling the increasing warmth between them. Think of this warmth as your healing energy, which you are able to hold right between your hands. Close your eyes. Think of positive energy and purpose.

- When your hands are warm with healing energy, place your fingers lightly at the top of your forehead. Close your eyes. Slowly and gently, move your fingers down over your face, over your closed eyes, over your mouth and chin, and slowly and lightly down your neck. Pretend you are slowly and gently tracing lines in the sand. Breathe in clean and soothing air.

- Imagine that your tired feelings, your stress and worries, are floating down and out with your fingers as they move. When you finish, shake your hands out gently to rid yourself of any remaining tension.

- Rub your hands together again to connect to a feeling of energy and healing. You may continue the massage by starting at the top of your head and move your hands and fingers slowly and lightly down over your neck and shoulders. Each time, as you finish, shake your hands out gently and remind yourself to release any remnants of tension or stress.

Make a time to practice the face massage this week. You may want to try it with your coach reading the instructions aloud to you. Write down your thoughts about how you felt after doing this technique:

Goal 32: Watch Your Body Language

When anxiety is very intense, your body and muscles respond with tension. This muscle tension can leave you feeling chilled, tight, and sore. It's often the case that body habits that develop as a reaction to frequent anxiety actually intensify the feeling of anxiety. Ask yourself and your coach if you have a tendency to do any of the following when you are feeling more anxious.

- **Closing your eyes.** Some people close their eyes when they feel afraid or nervous. This can make you feel much worse.

  Practice the Solution: Remind yourself to open your eyes and do deep breathing. You can loosen your muscles, get more oxygen, and think more clearly.

- **Moving your hands to your face.** This is a natural fear response, but can trigger more intense anxiety in relation to your everyday stress and worry.

Practice the Solution: Let your hands move away and fall lightly on your lap. Practice deep breathing. Say a positive affirmation to remind yourself that you are safe.

- **Wringing your hands.** You feel restless, nervous, or antsy.

Practice the Solution: Shrug your shoulders gently and let your shoulders release. Practice deep breathing. Think of letting all the muscles in your hands lengthen and loosen.

- **Your voice gets higher and you talk faster.** You feel overwhelmed by your negative, worried thoughts. You may even feel that you are losing control or that it is becoming difficult to breathe.

Practice the Solution: Slow down. Practice deep breathing for at least a few minutes. Start to talk slowly and deliberately, listening carefully to the tone of your voice. Reassure yourself that nothing has happened and that you are in control. Breathe.

- **You cry uncontrollably and frequently each day.** While crying is helpful to relieve stress and let go of intense emotion, frequent and uncontrollable crying can make you feel worse and be exhausting.

Practice the Solution: Open your eyes wide. Blink deliberately a few times. Practice slow, deep breathing for a few minutes. Open your mouth wide and stretch your jaw gently, then relax your mouth. Yawn. Focus on a neutral topic other than what you were crying about. Continue to focus on your breathing and loosening the muscles in your head and neck.

Discuss any changes in your body or presentation when you become anxious with your coach or other close friend or family member. Ask them to remind you to practice the solutions listed if they see you doing these behaviors. Remember, it takes practice and time to change a habit.

Goal 33: Sing Your Blues Away

Singing is a great stress reliever and requires that you practice deep breathing without even thinking about it. Think of a favorite song that gives you a good feeling. Songs from musicals are great choices. Choose one that is not too long or complicated. Your goal is to sing that song at least once a day for the next week. It's all right if you do not remember the words or you sing out of key. You can sing it anytime, when you are calm or even in the middle of the night when you feel nervous. (Give the other people in your home some earplugs.) You can sing it alone or ask other people to join you. The idea is to enjoy the song and breathe!

My song will be: _____

How I felt after singing: _____

_____

_____

Goal 34: Getting Physical

Anxiety is so strongly associated with physical feelings of tension and muscle soreness that it is a good idea to do some sort of physical exercise to release some of it. In addition to the ideas presented in chapter 8, consider the following exercises to incorporate into your week:

- **Walking.** The wonderful thing about walking and any other aerobic activity is that you have to breathe more deeply to do it. Some people prefer to walk instead of deep breathing. Get outside if you can, or walk indoors.

- **Dancing.** You don't have to be Fred Astaire or Ginger Rogers to enjoy dancing. You also do not have to have a partner or get dressed up to put on some music and move around your living room. Don't worry about what other people would think—do it for your own benefit.

- **Tai chi or qigong.** Both of these forms of exercise have become very popular among older adults. Research has shown that tai chi can reduce stress, increase physical strength, and improve balance and endurance. There is a sense of community when you take a class with other people. If you live in a community where tai chi is regularly practiced in public parks, go and join in. You can also practice alone in your own home with a video. See suggestions in the Resources section.

- **Sex.** Sexual activity is a natural stress reliever. Don't let outdated notions about older people being incapable of intimacy hold you back!

- **Swimming.** There is something about floating in water that is extremely relaxing. There are programs for seniors with swim hours and classes at many recreation centers as well as at some senior centers.

Goal 35: Your Relaxation Toolbox

Take a look around your house. There may be many things there that can give you a sense of calm but that you may not have thought of or noticed recently. It may be as easy as taking something off of a shelf and trying it again or finding a new use for something that you already have. Collect different tools for relaxation and keep them in a special drawer or box. This will make it easy for you to find them to practice with when you need them. Here are some ideas for your "toolbox":

- Seashells or smooth stones from a hike near a river. Items with appealing textures can help you connect physically and emotionally.

- A relaxation tape or soft instrumental music. There are some wonderful tapes to choose from. You may want to experiment or borrow one to find one that is most appealing to you. For example, you may find that you prefer either a male or female voice on the tape. Some people with hearing impairments find background music to be annoying. See a list of suggestions in the Resources section at the end of this book.

- Cut out pictures from magazines of beautiful and serene landscapes that resonate with your view of peacefulness. Put these on the wall or in a notebook that you can look at when you need to relax.

- Favorite bath salts for a warm relaxing soak in the tub can induce a greater state of calm, as can scented candles for use in any room.

- Write down a simple exercise routine that you can do. Keep it in your toolbox as a reminder.

- Collect your favorite aromas, perhaps bottles that you have not opened in a long time. Think about the pleasure and good thoughts that these scents can impart. As you grow older, you may have a reduced sense of smell. You may need to find fresh scents; you may discover that you respond to stronger aromas than in the past. Incorporate the use of scents with your practice of deep breathing and visualization to create a more powerful relaxation response.

- Watch or read a favorite comedy. Laughter is a great stress reliever. Purchase a favorite funny movie if possible or have a copy of the book handy. Or write a list of the most hilarious movies that you can think of so that you can rent one when you need a good belly laugh. You may not feel like laughing when you are depressed or anxious, but it may be just what you need.

- Make a squeeze ball. This is a fun tool to have that many occupational therapists use to build strength in the hands. Get a round, medium-sized balloon and fill with flour. (Attach a car oil funnel or other larger funnel to the open end of the balloon to pour flour in slowly; shake the flour down to pack it firmly. Push out any excess air and tie off the balloon.) When you feel stress, squeeze the ball gently. We carry a lot of tension in the muscles of our hands, and this exercise with the squeeze ball can be very soothing. Be careful, however, not to overdo. People with carpal tunnel syndrome or arthritis in their hands should limit the time that they do this exercise. Long, sharp fingernails can also cause a messy problem with this tool!

Anxiety is an uncomfortable and sometimes frightening experience, whether you have depression or not. Some anxiety is inevitable. But it does not have to take control of your life. By being creative and willing to try a variety of relaxation activities, you can get a handle on anxiety.

Chapter 8

Exercise and Nutrition for the Third Age

Exercise and nutrition are critically important tools for elevating your mood and managing your depression. Proper exercise and nutrition will keep you healthier, happier, and more independent as you age—and it is never too late to start.

Lorraine's Story

Lorraine is a petite, pretty woman who says with a laugh, "I look every bit of my eighty-two years." Lorraine was born and raised in the South and is a descendant of several generations of Southerners. She never worked, except to raise six children who she says, "were work enough for me, and I'm so proud of every one of them." Her husband was a successful businessman and their life together was happy through the years. Then one summer night Lorraine's eldest son, just shy of his fiftieth birthday, was killed in a car accident.

The shock and pain for the entire family was overwhelming, but with time, everyone was able to put their lives back together and move on. Except Lorraine. Lorraine had problems sleeping, she had no appetite, and she worried incessantly about her other children, fearing that another one of them would have some horrible accident. She lost weight and refused to go out of the house, except when absolutely necessary.

Lorraine's husband finally talked her into seeing the doctor, who diagnosed her with depression. He prescribed an antidepressant medication and told Lorraine that if her health did not improve, he would have to hospitalize her. He also recommended a therapist in town.

Lorraine was mortified at the thought of seeing a therapist, and was fearful that her friends would find out, but she decided that she had no choice but to get help. During one of her sessions, her therapist suggested that she take a group exercise class for seniors held at a local church. Lorraine's immediate reaction was, "I couldn't possibly exercise! It's just so tedious, and besides that, I'm too damn old for such silliness."

With the constant prodding of her therapist, Lorraine finally agreed to try the class. Her first day there, she was surprised to see that most of the ladies and men were as old as she was—and a couple of them were even older. The instructor took the time to give Lorraine specific instructions on how to get started; before the actual exercise began, the class was led in a series of gentle stretches. Then the music started. The tunes were from Lorraine's era, with a few contemporary songs thrown in. Everyone in the class was very supportive, and although Lorraine wasn't able to keep up with the rest of the class, she wasn't made to feel out of place. After she got home, she felt an unfamiliar exhilaration along with her usual tiredness.

Lorraine continued to attend the class weekly, and after about two months she started to notice her energy increase and her appetite improve. She felt stronger and more in control of her life, and even though she struggled with the painful thoughts and feelings of having lost her son, she was able to focus on something else. Lorraine was able to talk in therapy about how she realized now that her son would want her to be happy and healthy.

Lorraine attended her class with a fervor and commitment that had been missing in her life. She eventually was able to stop going to therapy, but continued to take her antidepressant medications. Lorraine not only resumed the activities she had given up, but did so with "more energy than I have had in years."

Exercise Is the Key to Better Aging

Establishing and maintaining overall health and wellness will help you stay independent and have enduring quality of life well into old age. As previously mentioned in chapter 1, depression is an illness that is associated with a variety of medical conditions. The healthier you stay, the more likely you are to not only possibly prevent a depressive episode, but to have the energy and resolve to recover from an episode should it occur.

Numerous medical and physical constraints may make it challenging for you to consider exercising. You may be in a wheelchair or be sight impaired, or have some other physical problem. We can't address all possible problems that require adaptation to some of the exercises we suggest in this chapter. However, you should be able to do some form of exercise regardless of your disability. There are "sit and be fit" exercises, videos, and special classes for stroke or heart attack victims. If you are willing to ask for help to investigate the possibilities, you should be able to dramatically improve your fitness.

Exercise, or more precisely, fitness, is generally thought of as having several important components. Each of these is necessary for overall fitness and health, although you may decide to gravitate toward one area more than another. Each of these types of exercise have both short- and long-term benefits that will also be mentioned.

- **Endurance Exercises:** These are exercises that increase your breathing and heart rate. The term "aerobic" is used to describe most endurance exercises. Some examples of endurance exercises are: walking at a brisk pace, running, swimming, tennis, raking leaves, dancing, shoveling, rowing, climbing stairs, and biking. Your heart, lungs, and circulatory systems stay healthier with endurance exercise. Endurance is necessary for many of the activities that you do daily to stay independent and self-sufficient: cleaning your house, climbing the stairs, gardening, grocery shopping, and keeping up with the grandkids.

- **Strength Exercises:** Strength exercises build muscle. Examples include: doing certain calisthenics, or using hand weights, milk jugs filled with sand, socks filled with beans, resistance bands, or strength training machines that you can buy or use in a health club. As you get older, you lose muscle mass unless you do strength exercises. Without adequate muscle and strength, you eventually would lose the ability to do even simple tasks of daily living. Getting up out of a chair, taking a shower, preparing a meal, going to the store, getting dressed—these all require muscle. Loss of muscle mass can result in a person becoming frail and needing nursing care because they can't take care of themselves any longer. You can increase your muscle at any age and improve your odds of staying independent.

- **Flexibility Exercises:** Keeping your body limber can help to prevent injuries from occurring. Stretching alone does not improve endurance and strength, but all of these put together can improve balance to prevent falls and minimize the risk of injury and illness. Types of stretching exercises that work well for older adults are tai chi, yoga, and other gentle stretching exercises that can be done at home with the help of a video or book.

- **Posture and Balance:** As you get older, you may find that your posture and walking have become more stooped. One study suggests that attitudes about being old can influence your posture and gait. One way to visualize a healthy posture is to imagine a string running from the top of your head up to the sky, pulling you tall. Walk like you're younger and hold your head high!

Exercise: Where You Are Now

Taking into consideration the components listed above, write down the exercise that you are doing currently. Think in terms of *activity level*. Although you may not be involved in a formalized exercise routine, you may still be quite active with activities such as gardening, housecleaning, caretaking, or playing with the grandkids.

_____

_____

_____

Now, rate your activity level on a scale of 1 to 5, with 5 being the most active time of your life. This will give you a better perspective on where you are now with your activity level.

1_____   2_____   3_____   4_____   5_____

Exercise Is Not for Sissies

The word exercise can mean very different things to different people. Some of you look at the word and think of aerobics classes or calisthenics. Others of you think of hard work, pain, or sacrifice—and believe exercise is something to be avoided. And still others of you may be marathon runners or swimmers with your own unique perspective on what exercise is and what it means to you, as well as how depression has impacted this important part of your life and well-being.

Your attitude toward exercise impacts your willingness to make this significant and necessary lifelong change. Being depressed makes it that much harder to consider starting or continuing to exercise for the rest of your life. There are many myths and misunderstandings about exercise and aging. Let's look at a few of the misconceptions and then state the reality.

- **I'm too old to get started at this point in my life.**
  You are *never* too old to add some exercise to your life. Studies have shown that people of any age, whether they are fifty-five or 105, have benefited from exercise. Many studies have shown that moderate strength training (weight lifting or other resistance training) can improve muscle strength dramatically in people in their nineties and beyond, thereby reducing the risk of falls and fractures and allowing increasing independence. With the proper instruction and the help of your doctor, you can begin some exercise at any age.

- **I have too many physical problems that keep me from exercising.**
  People with every known medical condition can and do exercise. This includes people who are in wheelchairs, or are blind, or have had strokes or any number of other serious medical problems. Depending what your medical condition is, you should be able to find help through your doctor or other health-care provider on what types of exercises would be safe and effective for you.

- **I don't know where to go or how to get started.**
  We will tell you where to go and how to get started later in this chapter. We will also refer you to some excellent resources on exercise that will provide many more specifics on this topic than we are able to provide in this chapter. It is possible for you to achieve a relatively high level of fitness without ever having to leave your home, but it is almost always preferable to access outside resources. The more activity you can manage, the better. By doing activities outside your home you are more likely to meet other people and have access to a wider variety of equipment, programs, classes, and support.

- **I'm afraid I will look silly.**
  Well, you might, but this is something you will just have to get over. Feeling self-conscious when starting an exercise program is common for people of all ages. As you become more accustomed to your routine, much of that feeling will subside. Remember that everyone starts at the same place: the beginning.

- **I might hurt myself.**
  Injury is always a risk with exercise, but there is far greater risk associated with not exercising. By following simple steps and taking reasonable precautions, you can minimize the risk of injury. Checking with your doctor and starting slowly will help. Remember that starting an exercise

program is a lifelong journey that takes place one step at a time. Be patient and be careful.

- **I'm too tired to exercise.**
  Being depressed can make it doubly difficult to get started with an exercise program. Depression can also make it hard to get back to an exercise regime that you have already started. Fatigue and lack of motivation are strong deterrents, but your energy and motivation will come back in time. Don't wait until you "feel better" before you begin to increase your activity level. You may experience some tiredness after you start to exercise, but eventually you should notice an increase in energy and endurance.

Exercise: Take Stock of Your Excuses

Take a moment to write down some of the reasons why you aren't exercising now and categorize them into the following areas. This will help you sort out what may seem like overwhelming problems in getting started.

Emotional: _____

Physical or Medical: _____

Attitudes: _____

Logistical: _____

Financial: _____

How Getting Physically Fit Will Improve Your Mental Attitude

Getting and staying physically fit as you age has so many advantages that it is important to enumerate them. In fact, not exercising has many risks associated with it. Keep in mind as you read this how critical it is as you age to stay independent and healthy. *Without good physical health and the ability to remain independent, your chances of keeping control over the quality and direction of your life are slim.* Feeling that you have some control over your health will give you more confidence to handle the stress and symptoms of your depression.

Exercise improves mood. Prolonged, continuous exercise contributes to an increase in the production and release of endorphins. Endorphins are neurotransmitters, (chemicals in the brain) that act as pain regulators and contribute to feelings of euphoria. You may have heard the term "runner's high." This refers to the feeling of well-being that many runners report having not only during their runs, but throughout the day. This feeling of well-being can occur with many other types of aerobic exercise as well. Exercise won't necessarily prevent you from getting depression, but it can help you to fight and perhaps reduce the symptoms.

Staying physically active and exercising regularly can help prevent or delay some diseases and disabilities. Exercise cuts your risk of dying. Rowe and Kahn (1998) state in *Successful Aging* that exercise can actually negate the adverse affects of smoking, high blood pressure, and high blood sugar. "This dominant effect of fitness over other risk factors, and its apparent effect as an antidote for other risk factors, makes physical fitness perhaps the single most important thing an older person can do to remain healthy" (p. 98). Exercise improves the efficiency of your heart, lungs, muscles, and bones. Rowe and Kahn also outline other benefits of exercises:

> Physical activity cuts the rate of coronary heart disease. . . . Exercise cuts the risk of getting hypertension in half and also helps lower existing high blood pressure. . . . An increase in physical activity protects against colon cancer. . . . Moderate exercise often relieves arthritis pain and disability. . . . Weight-bearing activity such as lifting weights, walking, or dancing is a potential means of counteracting age-related bone loss. . . . Exercise improves balance, which can cut the risk of falls. (pp. 108–10)

We have talked in chapter 1 about the relationship of depressive symptoms to disease and disability. Depression is a disease that affects the whole body.

Physical decline is not inevitable as you age. Of course there is some physical decline as you age, but much of that decline can be mitigated by exercise. We have talked about attitudes and aging and how your perception of what old age is can influence the decisions you make. The typical mindset about older adults and exercise has been shaped by the same attitudes that view old age as a time of decline and disability. Gradual physical decline leads to weakness, which contributes to more inactivity, which in turn creates more dependence on others, increased isolation, powerlessness, and further decline. You have more control over your health than you probably realize.

Exercise and a lifelong commitment to health will help you cope with the symptoms of depression. We have talked about how depression can sap your energy and drain away your motivation to complete even the easiest tasks. We have also discussed how important it is to stay mentally stimulated and socially active. Here are some ways exercise can help:

- **If you want to build more energy, you must do more than you feel like doing.** Initiating some physical activity will jump-start your energy. If you aren't ready to go full steam ahead with an exercise program, at least begin to increase your activity level by doing one or more of the following: stretch each morning before you start your day; do more around the house than you are accustomed to; start on a project that you have been putting off by taking small steps to get it accomplished; take short walks; work in the yard.

- **Many physical activities involve other people. Dance, tai chi, exercise classes, walking, golf, and many other exercises are often done with others.** As a bonus, group activities provide a chance to develop social connections while getting fit. Look for classes specifically designed for older adults through the resources we mention at the end of the book. You may find it much easier to adhere to an exercise routine if you have other people to motivate and inspire you. You might even consider asking one or more of your friends to join you in some activity.

- **Motivation can sometimes be elusive even under the best of circumstances.** If you wait for motivation to come knocking at your door, you will most likely have a very long wait. But you have more control over your motivation level than you think you do. Motivation is often born out of activity and involvement. Give yourself rewards for exercise goals you accomplish. Make signs or notes for yourself that you can place in conspicuous places to remind you of your exercise and fitness goals. Practice positive self-talk that reinforces your abilities and inspires you to action. Examples of this might be: "I can do whatever it takes to get healthy!" "I am a strong and capable person." "I will feel better if I just get started!" "I will give it my best effort and be satisfied with that."

- **Regular physical activity helps reduce stress. It also helps you to relax and feel less tense.** Many studies have confirmed what people who exercise have been saying for years. While exercise elevates your mood, it also helps your body to relax naturally and eases the mental strain of stress and worry. Anxiety and nervousness manifest themselves physically. Think of a time when you have been keyed up and worried. Adrenaline is pumping and you feel like jumping out of your skin. Exercise helps to release this tension naturally and can have the added benefit of clearing your mind.

- **Exercise improves your ability to fall asleep quickly and sleep well.** Regular physical activity makes the body tired naturally and helps you to sleep longer and more deeply without the aid of medications. Exercising just before bedtime can make it more difficult to fall asleep, so it may be better to complete your exercise two to three hours prior to bedtime.

- **Exercise helps to improve self-image.** When your mood, energy, and health improve, you feel better about yourself. As you gain more control and confidence in your ability to manage your own health, your self-esteem increases. Knowing that the choices you make will shape your life in positive ways empowers you to make those choices in the future with more confidence.

Taking the First Step

Before you make the first step to begin exercise, *make an appointment with your doctor to get a complete physical exam.* If your doctor tells you that you are too old to exercise, you may want to confer with another doctor who understands how critical exercise is for older adults.

The National Institutes of Health (NIH) states that for people with some conditions, *vigorous* exercise is dangerous and should be avoided. The definition of "vigorous exercise" depends on your current fitness level. For some of you "vigorous" will mean running and for others it will be walking a very short distance.

Getting started exercising is going to depend on a number of factors:

- your current fitness level

- whether you live in an urban or rural area

- your ability to access community resources

- your financial situation

- the amount of support you have from family and friends

Exercise: Investigating the Possibilities

Here are a number of ideas on where to go to get started. Check the box next to an idea that you are willing to try:

- ☐ Read everything you reasonably can about exercise and older adults. Refer to the end of the book for suggested reading. Much of the information is available online.

☐ Check with your local Area Agency on Aging or senior center to inquire about exercise classes for older adults. Your local senior center might offer classes.

☐ Investigate exercise videos for older adults at the library, online, or at your local video store.

☐ After doing some research, look into buying some exercise equipment you can use at home. You may opt for simple hand weights, or you may decide to purchase more elaborate exercise machines. A good place to start is in the yellow pages of the phone book under Exercise Equipment.

☐ Look into hiring a fitness professional who specializes in the needs of older adults. These include: doctors who specialize in sports medicine; physical therapists, and exercise physiologists. The American College of Sports Medicine (ACSM) trains and certifies people to work with older adults. Inquire at a health club, university, or your physician's office for one of these qualified individuals.

☐ Check into whether hospitals and health maintenance organizations in your area feature wellness centers that offer exercise programs.

☐ Ask to see if colleges and universities in your city have special exercise classes for older adults or conduct special studies on aging and exercise.

☐ Start your own program that you develop from the reading that you do. Make a calendar (see next section) and set achievable goals.

☐ Investigate city, county, regional, state, and national parks and recreation programs.

☐ Contact your local health clubs, YMCA, or YWCA

☐ Find out about community education programs. Universities and colleges often sponsor community programs that offer not only exercise classes but also a wide range of adult learning classes. State and local recreation programs often offer exercise and fitness programs as well.

☐ Contact your local public health office.

Get Your Mind on Your Health

We have talked briefly about how difficult and challenging it can be to begin or continue on the path to overall wellness. In addition to having depression, you may have numerous other challenges to beginning a fitness program, such as medical problems or difficulty in accessing transportation.

Exercise: Acknowledge Your Challenges

The prospect of getting started may seem overwhelming. It may take time, hard work, and lots of help, but you can and will take steps toward a healthier life. Say to yourself now that you accept the biggest challenge of all: *Taking control and taking charge of your health, now and forever.* Write down your challenges here:

1. _____

2. _____

3. _____

4. _____

5. _____

Exercise: Let Nothing Get in Your Way

Take a look at the challenges you listed above. Now problem-solve these barriers and write possible solutions to each of the ones you have listed above. Talk with your coach about your challenges and see if he or she has some ideas.

1. _____

2. _____

3. _____

4. _____

5. _____

How to Stay Motivated

The NIH offers the following advice on keeping and increasing your motivation. We have also added a few ideas of our own.

Ask someone to be your exercise buddy. Having someone to get started with you can help keep you on track and give you company while you exercise. If you aren't able to find someone to be your buddy, join a class or group.

Set a goal and decide on a reward that you will get when you reach it. Make sure that your reward doesn't negate the affects of the activity! Reward yourself with a movie, a new outfit, a long-distance phone call to one of your children, a new hairdo, or a manicure. You probably have other rewards in mind as well.

Give yourself physical activity homework assignments for the next day or next week. Use a calendar or chart to check off when you have completed a goal. Keep your goals reasonable and achievable.

Think of your exercise sessions as appointments, and mark them on your calendar. Don't let anything interfere with these appointments. Also make them specific, such as: "I will walk fifteen minutes tomorrow between the hours of 12:00 and 3:00 P.M." This way you will have made an appointment that can't be broken.

Keep a record or diary of what you do and the progress you make. By keeping track of what you do daily for activity, you can look back and see the progress that you have made. One of the symptoms of depression is negative thinking and poor self-esteem. Having a record of your gains will give you a more accurate perspective on the positive efforts you are making.

Understand that there will be times when you don't make progress and that you are still benefiting from your activities. This can be said of almost any aspect of recovery from depression, whether it is therapy, group support, self-help efforts, nutrition, or exercise. If you are making an effort to improve your health, you will not always see or feel immediate benefits. There may be times when you actually take a couple of steps back. Have faith that you will rebound and move forward again. If you are struggling with the feeling that you aren't making progress, talk this over with your coach to get a more realistic view of how you are doing. Be patient and give yourself credit for the effort you are making.

Plan ahead for vacations or houseguests. Know in advance how you will adapt. Working on recovering from depression is a full-time job. Devotion and commitment to your health takes time, focus, and energy, qualities that may be in short supply when you are depressed. Many people may not understand or empathize with what you are going through and resent the time you are taking away from family and other responsibilities to focus on what you need. People close to you may view your dedication to health as selfish or self-centered. Making a commitment to your mental, physical, and emotional health is not selfish—it is a priority. When you have planned during your day to exercise, nothing short of illness or some other critical, pressing problem should interfere. If you don't make your health a priority, then any number of other obligations and responsibilities will distract you from your mission to improve your health. Talk to people about how important it is to your recovery to keep your exercise appointment. If they don't support you, it's probably because they wish they had your dedication.

Don't compare yourself to other people. Where you are in your exercise program is where you need to be. This is harder than it sounds. It is human nature to compare ourselves to others. Again, remember that everyone else you see started where you did, at the beginning. Regardless of how little it seems like you are doing or how small your steps are, have faith that you are on the right path—one that will improve your life in immeasurable ways.

If you are having a particularly bad day, don't use that as an excuse not to exercise. Chances are good that you will feel better if you go ahead and exercise as planned. If you are ill or injured, it is best to take a day or more off from your exercise routine. But if you "just don't feel like it," that is not a good enough excuse. Considering that a major symptom of depression is apathy and fatigue, then this excuse is likely to come up fairly frequently. Recognize it for what it is—an opportunity to sabotage your efforts. Remain firm in your resolve to push yourself past your negative thoughts.

Visualize yourself as an active person. Visualization has been used for years as an effective method of improving performance. This technique can be applied to almost any aspect of your life. With respect to depression, you can visualize yourself as a positive, happy, optimistic person. If you have a fitness or health goal, imagine that you have reached it. Visualize what you look and feel like. See yourself as a healthy, glowing person with much to look forward to.

Watch less TV and do something active instead. When your energy is drained and your motivation is low, it is easy to fall into a cycle of inactivity and apathy. Notice your self-defeating behaviors and limit those activities. If necessary, put a note of caution on the TV, refrigerator, or couch!

It's Never Too Late: Simple Exercise Tips and Goals

It is beyond the scope of this book to give detailed exercise instruction, so we will refer you to information on exercise and older adults that you can consult to begin your exercise. To start with, here's some advice on pacing yourself: "It is important to start out at a level that you can manage and work your way up gradually. If you do too much too quickly, you can damage your muscles and tissues. Starting out with one or two types of exercises that you really can manage and that you really can fit into your schedule, then adding more as you adjust, is one way of ensuring that you will stick with it" (The National Institutes of Health 2001, p. 3). For more information on how to obtain a copy of *Exercise: A Guide from the National Institute on Aging* from NIH, see the Resources section.

This advice about beginning gradually is crucial—don't rush yourself. Always keep in mind that doing some exercise is better than doing none at all. A possible schedule to begin with is shown below. You can choose what types of exercises to do in each category, and you may decide to do different exercises on different days.

Sample Exercise Schedule

Adapt and change this schedule to meet your needs. Check with your doctor before embarking on any exercise program.

Week One

Monday	Tuesday	Wednesday	Thursday	Friday	Saturday	Sunday
Stretching: 5–10 minutes	Warm-up & Endurance: 5 minutes each	Strength Training: 15 minutes	Endurance & Stretching: 5 minutes each	Strength: 15 minutes	Warm-up & Endurance: 5 minutes each	Rest

Week Two

Monday	Tuesday	Wednesday	Thursday	Friday	Saturday	Sunday
Stretching: 10 minutes	Warm-up: 5 minutes	Strength: 15 minutes	Stretching: 10 minutes	Strength: 15 minutes	Warm-up: 5 minutes	Rest
	Endurance: 10 minutes		Endurance: 10 minutes		Endurance: 10 minutes	

Week Three

Monday	Tuesday	Wednesday	Thursday	Friday	Saturday	Sunday
Stretching: 10 minutes	Warm-up: 5 minutes	Strength: 15 minutes	Stretching: 10 minutes	Strength: 15–20 minutes	Warm-up: 5 minutes	Rest
	Endurance: 15 minutes		Endurance: 15 minutes		Endurance: 15 minutes	

Week Four

Monday	Tuesday	Wednesday	Thursday	Friday	Saturday	Sunday
Stretching: 10–15 minutes	Warm-up: 5 minutes	Strength: 15–20 minutes	Stretching: 10–15 minutes	Strength: 15–20 minutes	Warm-up: 5 minutes	Rest
	Endurance: 20 minutes		Endurance: 20 minutes		Endurance: 20 minutes	

Goal 36: Deciding What to Do

Finding the type of endurance exercise that you like may be a matter of trial and error. Some people love to swim and others wouldn't think of getting in a pool. Whatever kind of exercise you choose, think of the commitment as one that you make for a lifetime.

Combine endurance, strength, and stretching for a complete approach to life-long fitness. You will be rewarded with the skills and confidence to take charge of your mental, physical, and emotional well-being. Take a moment to commit to beginning an exercise schedule. One thing that might help you get started is to take a walk in your neighborhood and think about what you plan to do. You may find that walking is what suits you best! State here what you plan to do, how you plan to do it, and where.

Type of exercise I will do: _____

How I will begin: _____

Where I will do my exercise: _____

Date started: _____

If you had already been exercising but stopped due to depression, make an agreement with yourself to get started again by a certain date. Keep your expectations reasonable and start back slowly.

I will start my exercise program again by: _____

_____

Goal 37: Motivation Is the Key

Look back over the motivational suggestions we made earlier in the chapter. Identify what you think will work best to keep you on track with your exercise program. You may want to consider something small like cutting back on TV watching, or visualizing yourself as an active vibrant person. Choose something you feel confident you can achieve.

My motivational tools:

_____

_____

_____

Great! You are on your way to a healthier you.

Now, let's talk about how good nutrition can keep your body healthy and your mind clear.

Nutrition: You Are What You Eat

Few topics occupy the media or our thoughts more than food. The weight-loss industry in this country is a multibillion dollar industry. New research seems to come out daily that is often more confusing than it is illuminating. But one thing we do know is that we Americans are dying from heart disease, cancer, diabetes, and obesity at alarming rates.

The other thing we know is that evidence continues to build that the foods we eat play a role in preventing these diseases. There are some basic guidelines you can follow to fight disease and improve your health, giving you the energy and vitality necessary to do the things you want to do.

When You Don't Feel Like Eating

Most people who are depressed report changes in their appetite. The majority of these people say that they lose their appetite when they are depressed, although some report an increase in appetite. You have probably noticed some change in your eating habits since being depressed. This is not unusual, but can be cause for concern. Proper nutrition is a necessary component of your recovery and efforts to improve your overall health.

Possible changes that could be related to diet include:

- weight loss

- weight gain

- nausea after eating

- a tendency to eat foods with poor nutritional value such as sweets, foods high in fat

- increasing feelings of fatigue

- dizziness

- confusion

The fact is, you may just not feel like eating when you are depressed, which leads to more weakness and fatigue. You need food for fuel. Your mind and body must have proper nutrition to function properly, and you need your mind and body to help you recover from depression.

We have talked about how important exercise is when recovering from depression. Over time, men and women lose muscle mass. As you lose muscle mass, you require fewer calories for your body to perform its basic functions. Many older adults skip out on exercise and continue to eat the way they did when they were young. The result is increasing weight over the years. But by exercising you can build your muscle mass and increase or maintain your metabolism.

Exercise: Keeping Track of What You Eat

You will feel better if you eat a healthy diet, and you will have more energy to stay active, involved, and motivated. Let's get started by taking a look at what you are eating now. Be honest and write down what your diet consists of currently. Keep track of everything you eat over the next three days, or if you can remember, write down what you have eaten over the last three days.

Food Diary

Day One	Day Two	Day Three
Breakfast:	Breakfast:	Breakfast:
Lunch:	Lunch:	Lunch:
Dinner:	Dinner:	Dinner:
Glasses of water:	Glasses of water:	Glasses of water:
Snacks:	Snacks:	Snacks:

Now, evaluate as best you can, how depression is affecting your appetite. Notice how food tastes and smells. Have you lost some of your taste sensation? Does food smell good to you? Depression and antidepressant medications can affect your sense of taste.

How to Eat Well

Many organizations, including the American Heart Association, American Cancer Society, American Dietetic Association, American Society for Clinical Nutrition, and the National Institutes of Health all agree that the same healthy diet can help prevent chronic illnesses and keep your body and mind functioning optimally. There are of course exceptions to this diet if you have restrictions due to certain health conditions.

The diet these organizations recommend is described in the U.S. Dietary Guidelines and the Food Guide Pyramid—rich in plant foods (grains, beans, fruits, and vegetables) and low in fat. Although the Food Guide Pyramid has come under criticism from a number of groups, it is generally accepted today as the best guide to a healthy diet. If you use the Food Guide Pyramid as a guideline, you will be following a balanced diet and may be helping to prevent or delay some of the diseases associated with growing older. (See the Food Pyramid below).

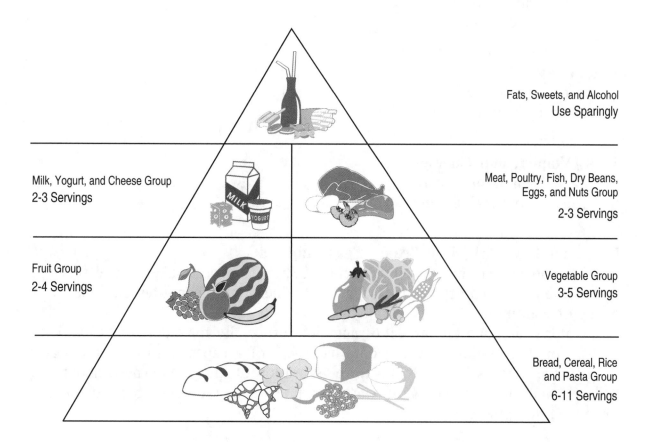

Fats, Sweets, and Alcohol
Use Sparingly

Milk, Yogurt, and Cheese Group
2-3 Servings

Meat, Poultry, Fish, Dry Beans, Eggs, and Nuts Group
2-3 Servings

Fruit Group
2-4 Servings

Vegetable Group
3-5 Servings

Bread, Cereal, Rice and Pasta Group
6-11 Servings

Serving Sizes Will Keep You on Track

Looking at the pyramid, you will see that your biggest calorie intake each day should come from grains, and the smallest amount should come from fats, oils, and sweets. The guidelines put a heavier emphasis on vegetables and fruits, and less on meat and dairy products.

Below are some examples of a serving size:

Grains
1 slice of bread
½ cup of cooked rice or pasta
½ cup of cooked cereal
1 ounce of ready-to-eat cereal

Fruits
1 piece of fruit
1 melon wedge
¾ cup fruit juice
½ cup canned fruit
½ cup dried fruit

Vegetables
½ cup of chopped raw or cooked vegetables
1 cup of leafy raw vegetables

Milk, Yogurt, and Cheese
1 cup of milk or yogurt
1½ to 2 ounces of cheese

Meat, Poultry, Fish, Dry Beans, Eggs, and Nuts
For cooked lean meat, poultry, or fish, 2 to 3 ounces make up one serving. A half cup of cooked dry beans, 1 egg, or 2 tablespoons peanut butter counts as 1 ounce of lean meat.

Water is an important aspect of nutrition, especially for older adults, who are at risk for dehydration. Older people have less of a capacity to conserve water through the kidneys, as well as a lower sensation of thirst. You need about one and one half to two quarts of water or juice a day unless your doctor has instructed you otherwise.

Goal 38: Changing the Way You View Your Diet

Now take a look at your three-day diet. Look at the food pyramid and compare your diet with the suggested types and amounts of foods listed there. What are some changes you can make to improve the way you eat? Look through your refrigerator and cupboards and compare what you see to what the food pyramid says you should have. Perhaps you need more fruits and vegetables or are lacking legumes and pasta.

What are you missing in your diet, and what are some items that you can add to your grocery list?

_____

_____

_____

As you consider adding some items to your diet, follow these tips:

- Pay special attention to getting variety in your diet.

- Try some foods you have never had before.

- Avoid prepared foods that are typically high in fat and sodium.

- Experiment a little. Focus on fresh foods and grains.

One good place to begin in changing your diet is to make a grocery list of the items on the food pyramid. Here are some other helpful tips:

- **Drink water first thing in the morning after you get up.** Leave yourself a note someplace conspicuous that reminds you to drink more water.

- **Keep healthy foods in the house, not unhealthy ones.** If you have unhealthy foods in the house, you are more likely to eat them.

- **Keep a copy of the food pyramid in a visible place.**

- **If you are losing weight due to loss of appetite, monitor your weight and try to eat more than you want to of the healthy foods on the pyramid.**

- **Eat a good breakfast.** This will start your day off right, and give you the energy you need throughout the day.

- **Stay away from diet pills and other risky diet gimmicks.** If you need to lose weight, do so with an exercise program that includes a healthy diet.

Goal 39: Making Dietary Changes to Feel Better

Considering the above list of suggestions, think about other improvements you can make in your diet and list them here:

_____

_____

_____

_____

_____

Vitamin Supplements: To Take or Not to Take

Whether to take vitamin supplements is a hotly debated topic, one that the vitamin marketing industry takes enormous financial advantage of, sometimes at the expense of older adults who simply cannot afford or don't need vitamins.

Another consideration when deciding whether to take vitamins or not, are the new kinds of supplements that are continuously promoted to improve everything from energy and sexual functioning to strength and memory. Many of these supplements have not been shown to do what they purport and may even be unsafe. If a supplement sounds too good to be true, it probably is.

According to the National Institutes of Health (2001), supplements can be helpful for some older adults who aren't able to get all the nutrients they need from the food they eat. A balanced diet based on the food pyramid is the best way to get all the vitamins and minerals you need. There are of course physician-detected exceptions in cases where you may have a specific imbalance or deficiency that requires supplementation. Please refer to the nutrition resources at the end of this book to get more information on vitamins and aging.

Before making a decision about whether to take vitamin supplements or what kind, check with your doctor. There may be no need to spend money on expensive supplements if you are getting most of the nutrients you need from a well-balanced, healthy diet.

Your Diet Can Make You Sick

You may be very confused by the seemingly conflicting reports you've heard about diet and disease. One minute you are told that butter is "bad" for you, and then information comes out that butter may be better than margarine. Despite these contradictions, there are some well-established associations that can be made between diet and disease. Here are a few of them:

Heart Disease

This is the number one killer of men and women in the U.S. Atherosclerosis, the underlying condition, is largely a result of dietary factors. Vascular disease, another major killer, is also linked to diet.

- Too much saturated and *trans* fat and cholesterol (largely from meat, dairy products, pastries, and eggs) raise blood cholesterol.

- Too many calories lead to obesity.

- Too little fiber, folate, and omega-3 fatty acids (like the fat in fish) and antioxidants (like vitamin E) leave the heart unprotected.

- Obesity, lack of exercise, excess alcohol, and insufficient potassium and magnesium raise blood pressure.

- Keeping your blood pressure on the low end of the normal range (partially achieved through diet) can protect against stroke.

Diabetes

The rates are climbing worldwide. The most important cause of diabetes is obesity.

- Obesity is more closely linked to diabetes than any other health problem.

- A sedentary lifestyle is also a risk factor.

- Some studies have shown that foods high in fiber may help prevent the disease.

Colon and Rectal Cancer

If you are not a smoker, the cancer most likely to kill you, other than breast or prostate, is cancer of the colon or rectum.

- Avoiding excess weight around the waist, increasing physical activity, and eating more fruits and vegetables can reduce your risk.

- Getting sufficient calcium and limiting red meat or saturated fat has a small reduction in risk associated with it.

- Starting at age fifty, getting a colonoscopy every ten years reduces risk.

Osteoporosis

One in two women and one in eight men over age fifty will fracture a bone because of osteoporosis in his or her lifetime, according to the National Osteoporosis Foundation (2001).

- Consuming adequate calcium and vitamin D lowers fracture rates in older people.

- Calcium appears to promote the positive effect of exercise and estrogen on bone.

- Exercise that is fully weight bearing—that is, standing—can strengthen bones if done in conjunction with calcium intake.

- Vitamin D aids in the absorption of calcium.

There are many other studies that have found varying degrees of association between diet and disease. Some of the diseases that have been and are currently being studied in relationship to diet are: breast cancer, arthritis, prostate cancer, Alzheimer's disease, and others. Don't get lost in the details of diet and vitamin supplements. Keep it simple and basic: Eat a well-balanced diet predicated on the Food Pyramid. Attend to any dietary restrictions that your doctor recommends. Stay away from supplements that make unsubstantiated dietary claims.

The Foundations of a Healthy Mind and Body

The connection between your mind and body is irrefutable. So are the benefits of diet and exercise. Aging may make it harder to stay active, independent, and healthy by virtue of the additional stress typically associated with growing older. However, we now know that many of what were once considered "inevitable" results of aging can be mitigated and even prevented through the lifestyle choices you make.

Depression and anxiety can take a tremendous toll on your body and mind. They can sap your mind's willpower and compromise your body's strength and resiliency. Making choices that improve your chances of staying healthy and strong will help you to recover more quickly. Additionally, these lifelong commitments to your health and independence will serve you well in your future endeavor to prevent relapse and create the life you want.

Chapter 9

Mind Over Medical
When Your Health Problems
Are a Barrier to Recovery

Many older adults feel betrayed by their health at a time when they had hoped to enjoy their lives. Combined with depression, chronic illness can lead to greater hopelessness. There is no way to eliminate the pain of illness, but every day, millions of people find ways to live with health changes and find contentment and richness in their lives. In this chapter, you will learn how to strengthen your attitude to effectively manage depression that coexists with other conditions.

Maureen's Story

To Maureen, tennis is "a game for life." "I've been involved with tennis since I was a girl growing up in Michigan. I've always been one to pick up a game when I'm traveling, with people I don't know. I just have such a love for it." Maureen had always been single and very involved in a business that required her to travel much of the year. "I was a regular maverick, but it suited me." When Maureen was seventy-two, she had a massive stroke. Suddenly, her life was turned upside down. She went through months of rehabilitation, but she could only walk a short distance with a walker and felt more secure with a wheelchair. Her left side was weak and she was afraid that she would fall down anytime that she tried to stand up. Her speech was slow and it was difficult for her to speak loudly enough for others to hear her. "After a while, I stopped trying. I just stopped talking."

Two years later, Maureen became severely depressed. "I thought that my life was over. I couldn't do the things that I wanted. I couldn't travel, I couldn't play tennis. I didn't want to be around my friends because it was such a nuisance to go anywhere with the walker. I didn't want to be a bother to them. I started to think about death a lot, that I would be better off if I just could go to sleep and never wake up."

A visiting nurse talked to Maureen about her depression and persuaded her to go to a therapist. The therapist encouraged Maureen to talk about all of her feelings. "I began to realize how mad I was that this had happened to me. I mean, I smoked for a while, but quit years ago. I tried to eat right and get exercise, and look what happened!" Maureen also talked to the therapist about how fearful she had become about falling. She admitted that she was so afraid that she avoided going anywhere. The therapist recommended that Maureen get more physical therapy and start to try to do some simple activities outside of her home. The first week, Maureen went to her front porch and sat down and then came back inside. "It sounds pretty easy for someone else, but it was terrifying for me. But I started to feel more daring after that." Maureen eventually started to call her old friends. They were glad to hear from her and very willing to help her with getting out of her house. The physical therapist showed Maureen some exercises to help stabilize her balance and encouraged her to walk more frequently. "I began to feel less reliant on the wheelchair. I could move further away from it each day."

Now, Maureen gets transportation to the senior center and enjoys having lunch with her friends there several times a week. She has met a woman there who is a bit younger and loves to travel also. They are planning a trip together to Florida next winter. "Louise is willing to put up with my slowness, and she is able to help me out if I need it." The best part is that Maureen is hanging out at the tennis courts again. "I go hit the backboard a little bit, not much so far. I like the feel of the racquet in my hand. I hang onto my walker and the young guy in the pro shop comes out to look in on me once in a while. But I love to be there, to smell the courts and hear the balls bouncing. I come out to watch the league matches. I'm turning into a great spectator. I love this game."

When Your Health Lets You Down

People of all ages dread the idea of their health failing. For older adults with chronic or debilitating illness, the idea of their "golden years" sounds like a cruel joke. Many people equate old age with illness. While normal aging is not synonymous with poor health, lifelong factors can contribute to greater vulnerability to illness among older adults. While some illnesses can start earlier in life, they seem to be particularly disruptive to those who have not had previous problems with their health. Illness can be chronic, meaning that you will continue to have it and need treatment for it and that it can progress to a more serious level. An example of this is diabetes. An illness can also be terminal, meaning that it generally progresses and, if not treated, can result in death. Cancer fits into this category.

The emotional impact of such illnesses is tremendous. Dealing with illness and pain can wreak havoc on your attitude toward life and what it means to you. While some people struggle initially with their circumstances and then find ways to accept their condition, others feel more and more hopeless. Hopelessness is a symptom of depression and can lead to suicidal thoughts and behavior. You may find yourself questioning your religious beliefs and feel guilty about doing so. You might feel like giving up and feel that the illness has taken over your life. Many older people relate that their first episode of depression occurred following the development of physical health problems.

Dealing directly with depression is a key factor in getting well. At the same time that you are taking control of your emotional health, you can adjust your attitude toward your physical health. While you must be realistic about the impact of certain illnesses on your life, you can also make proactive decisions on how you will manage. Many people who learn about an illness or experience the sudden onset of a condition do not get all the information that they need to cope adequately. Or you may have assumptions about your health outcomes that are not entirely true.

Exercise: Learn About Your Health

Write down the questions that you have about your condition so that you can ask your health-care provider the next time that you see them. Some doctors have extra appointment time available on request for consultation. Write down any questions, even if you think you should already know the answer.

_____

_____

_____

_____

Exercise: Black-and-White Thinking

When given bad news, you may start looking at the world in terms of polar opposites. With this kind of thinking, you think that you are either healthy and have no illnesses or that you are ill and doomed to live a life of misery. With black-and-white thinking, you tend to be undone by even small changes in your life or health. You have a hard time accepting that you can live with the condition that you have.

To move beyond black-and-white thinking, you must look for the degrees of gray in between. One way to cope more effectively with an illness is to examine how flexible your thinking is about the illness and its meaning in your life. Answer the following questions:

Do you think that your life is over because of <u>(name of illness)</u>? Why or why not?

_____

Are there possibilities for improvement in your condition?

_____

Is it possible that you could manage your condition in a more effective way?

_____

_____

Attitude Adjustment

Learning more about your attitude toward your health can help you find the vulnerable spots in your thinking. When we are ill, we begin to feel a lack of control over life. Some "attitude adjustments" can decrease the feeling of loss of control and allow you to feel more in charge. You might try one or more of these thinking strategies:

• Adopt a "wait and see" stance rather than deciding that your life is over.

- Allow that there will be phases to the illness and that you will experience ups and downs.

- Keep your mind open for improvements rather than ruling out the possibility. You may not be able to reverse a condition, but new treatments may be developed that will lessen your discomfort.

- Be insistent on living your life as much as possible the way you want to.

How You Do the Things You Do

One of the primary concerns when you become ill is how much it will alter the way you live your life. Will you be able to go places? Will you be able to get your groceries yourself? Will you be able to do the simple, private everyday tasks on your own, such as dressing, bathing, and even going to the toilet? Will you be able to see, hear, and communicate with others?

The way you do things and your ability to do them is referred to as *functioning*. How an illness affects your level of functioning is sometimes obvious to you and sometimes takes time to fully understand. A change in your level of functioning can mean the difference between doing something independently and needing someone or something to help you do it. Your functioning can be impaired temporarily or permanently.

Exercise: A Checklist for What You Do Now

Let's assess how you are doing the things that you do now. The following is a checklist of ordinary daily tasks. Place a check in the appropriate box indicating whether you do the specific task without assistance, with some assistance, or only with assistance. Also, assess if this is a temporary or permanent situation.

Daily Task Checklist

Task	No Assistance	Some Assistance	Only with Assistance	Permanent or Temporary
Bathing				
Dressing				
Going to the Toilet				

Task	No Assistance	Some Assistance	Only with Assistance	Permanent or Temporary
Getting Up from a Chair or Bed to Standing				
Managing Incontinence				
Eating				
Using the Phone				
Shopping				
Food Preparation				
Housekeeping				
Laundry				
Transportation				
Managing your Medications				
Managing Your Money				
Doing Leisure Activities				

Exercise: How Do You Feel About What You Are Doing?

When you have both depression and a medical condition, it can be hard to tell whether you have changed how you are functioning solely because of physical restrictions or because of the feeling of hopelessness and fatigue that depression brings with it. This becomes a crucial question to ask yourself. The influence of depression on the ability to overcome physical illnesses such as heart disease, stroke, and diabetes has been well studied. The findings are clear: Depression can make your overall health worse. How does your depression make it harder for you to push yourself to do things for yourself since dealing with a medical illness?

_____

_____

_____

═══════════════════════════════

═══════════════════════════════

Exercise: Watch Out for Independence Zappers!

Sometimes, after an illness or a hospitalization, well-meaning people around you get into a routine of assisting you and keep doing so even after you no longer need help. You may become accustomed to this and wonder why you should bother doing things for yourself again. But doing less than you are able has negative implications for you both physically and emotionally. Are there activities on the checklist above that you are getting assistance with that you would really like to (or should) return to doing more on your own?

_____

_____

_____

Sometimes, this situation is a result of someone who, with good intentions, wants to help you in your daily life. However, as mentioned, you need to be doing as much as you can for yourself. Think of ways that you can discuss the issue with this person and make a plan for you to slowly begin to do the task more on your own. Write down your ideas here and, if it helps, practice saying them out loud with your coach.

_____

_____

_____

═══════════════════════════════

Graciela's Story

Graciela has a hard time believing what she has been through in the last two years. "I always thought of myself as someone with pretty good health. Even though I have had diabetes for many years, I have done everything that I can to take care of myself and do the right thing." Her health changed when she started to have heart problems. She had to have bypass surgery about two years ago, and that's when her troubles began. Graciela had an infection following her surgery, resulting in a prolonged hospital stay and a difficult recovery period.

Though she had lived independently prior to this, Graciela moved in with her daughter and her family after getting out of a skilled nursing home. She was very weak and what was worse was that she was afraid. "I had always been a pretty confident person in my life. But I felt really afraid of this. I felt like I was waiting for the other shoe to drop." Her daughter, Robin, was also shaken by the change in her mother. She took her in and was determined to care for her in every way. Robin made her mother's bed, washed her clothes, and gave her backrubs at night. She didn't want her mother to lift a finger. Though Graciela was known for her skill in the kitchen, Robin insisted that she take it easy and allow her daughter to cook. Robin cooked for her whole family, including several school-age kids. "They could eat pizza every night, and my grandkids don't particularly like the vegetables that I do. But it's not easy to have two cooks in the kitchen."

Graciela spent a lot of time in her room. She felt so tired and weak. At first she felt bad about being waited on, but after a while she doubted that she could do the things that she had done before. "I started to feel really bad about myself. I wondered what I was still living for." Graciela talked to her doctor about feeling depressed and he started her on an antidepressant. Graciela also talked to a good friend of hers about what she was feeling. "My friend had gone through depression and she insisted that I needed to get out more. She came over to take me out and saw how Robin was doing everything for me. She talked to me about this at lunch and told me that I needed to be doing more for myself. I was sort of mad at her at first but later I got to thinking she was right." Graciela worked up her courage to talk to her daughter and Robin agreed that Graciela was not making the progress, physically or mentally, that she should. They came up with a plan for Graciela to start with some small tasks, such as making her bed, and then build on that each week by adding more activities and tasks. After a few weeks, Graciela made a simple meal for Robin and her family. Everyone, including Graciela, enjoyed it. "I won't be making meals every night. And Robin still does the shopping for me. But I am doing what I can, and that makes me feel better."

Exercise: Looking at Yourself in a Different Light

Picture a younger person whom you know, in their twenties or thirties, a friend or a relative. Imagine if that younger person had the same medical issue that you do. What would your advice be for that person and how would you want them to manage their condition?

_____

_____

_____

Would you handle your own medical condition differently if you were younger? Has your attitude about aging influenced your will to get better? Why or why not?

_____

_____

_____

_____

_____

_____

Getting Creative: Do Things in a New Way

As you know from reading earlier chapters of this book, it is imperative to be as active and out in the world as much as you can. This is a key factor in your healing process from depression. Having a physical condition that makes it difficult or painful for you to leave the house can make you feel like your life is over. While there might be factors that impede your getting around, it might still be possible for you to do some activities that you have given up on.

We will talk about some general areas of physical health changes and how some older adults have managed them. Rather than attempt to compile a list of all the possible medical conditions that you could have, we will consider areas of functioning that might be altered by physical problems. We will give examples of how other older adults have coped. We will not describe solutions for every problem, but rather create a starting point for you to look at your own challenges. Then you can start to come up with solutions that will work for you. As you read about how other people have handled certain situations, reflect on your own circumstances.

We have encountered many people who, in spite of medical conditions and depression, are involved and engaged in their lives. Their ability to come up with creative ways to solve the problems related to their health is tied to a decision and a desire to be problem solvers. This means that a solution may not be immediately obvious but that with some persistence, it can be found.

Consider the following areas of functioning:

Continence

Continence refers to the ability to control the elimination of urine (bladder continence) or stool (bowel continence) from your body. Incontinence of either urine or stool indicates a change in muscle control. The causes are numerous and can include prostate problems, the after-effects of surgery such as hysterectomy, or neurological damage from a stroke. Problems with continence create both embarrassment and fear for many people at any age.

If you have depression, incontinence can bring your self-esteem down further. Many older adults, with or without depression, confess that anxiety about accidents outside of home restricts them from going out. But, generally, incontinence is a condition that can be managed.

One Person's Solution

Al was admired by his friends for his sense of humor and well known as a snappy dresser. He had some wonderful suits and in spite of today's more casual standards, would dress stylishly for lunches out with his friends at the senior center. Al had a stroke several years ago and later dealt with intense depression. After getting treatment for depression, he faced the need to go out again and be with his friends. "I realized that a big part of why I was shunning my friends was because of incontinence. I realized that I could not let that hold me back from doing what I love to do best—which is to mix and mingle with my friends—any longer." Al confided in his grandson and they came up with an idea. Al would carry some extra pads inside his suit jacket pocket, and if he wanted to be out longer, he would bring his briefcase, in which he carried some extra clothes and supplies. "My grandson wanted to lend me his backpack. But the briefcase suits my style and I feel prepared. That helps me feel more at ease."

Respiratory Conditions

There are numerous chronic respiratory conditions that older people face: asthma, bronchitis, emphysema, and chronic obstructive pulmonary disease, as well as problems caused by allergies. Because these illnesses are associated with shortness of breath, they are particularly troublesome for people with anxiety and can trigger intense feelings of fear.

One Person's Solution

Eleanor had never been a smoker, but her deceased husband, Leo, had been a heavy smoker. The years of exposure to secondhand smoke left Eleanor with emphysema; eventually she had to wear oxygen to do her everyday tasks. When she was dealing with depression a few years ago, she became reclusive and anxious. She only felt safe within her own home, and besides, she detested carrying the oxygen tank with her. "All those tanks and pressure gauges made me a nervous wreck." Eleanor would defer all of her shopping to her niece, who brought her groceries once a week. But Eleanor realized that she really missed going to the nearby market and chatting with the clerk at the bakery counter. She decided to take action. She called her oxygen supplier and told him what her fears were about her equipment. He suggested that she try one of the smaller portable models with a conserving device. He came out to her home and showed her how she could carry this over her shoulder and he spent time teaching her how to operate it. Eleanor took notes and practiced turning the unit off and on. She also practiced carrying the unit around her house so that she could get used to it before she ventured out. "Now I get out and I feel like I am a part of the world. I'm not going to shop till I drop, but I feel a lot better when I can enjoy going through the store and see for myself what is there."

Chronic Pain

Many illnesses and injuries over a lifetime can result in ongoing, chronic pain. Arthritis, lupus, gout, and any number of back injuries can be the culprit. Chronic pain can be debilitating not only physically, but emotionally as well. Many people with chronic pain struggle with feelings of hopelessness. You can also get caught in a cycle where you anticipate pain to come and feel increasingly anxious. When you are depressed or anxiety is high, it seems to intensify your sensitivity to the feeling of pain. If you are dealing with chronic pain, review the chapter on anxiety carefully.

One Person's Solution

Norma was always the "gatherer" in her family: she organized the family reunions and consulted with far-flung family members to coordinate their schedules for these events. When she was in her early sixties, Norma developed severe arthritis and chronic pain in her back. There was little that her doctors could do, and pain relievers didn't seem to help. Norma was overcome with feelings of hopelessness and helplessness. She could not decide which was the worst part of the day: dealing with the discomfort of getting up and struggling to do the simplest things, or the nights when she lay awake comparing the pain to the agony of the night before.

Finally, a cousin of Norma's urged her to go to a therapist that she had gone to for depression. Norma talked about the terrible fear of the pain, and the therapist worked with Norma about how her negative thoughts were intensifying her pain. "My hopeless thoughts were like a magnifying glass, making my pain all the worse." Norma began to practice relaxation exercises and, with the therapist's encouragement, started to focus on her true interests again. Norma is back to phoning family members, and they are planning a reunion in the Midwest this summer. "Of course, the pain is still there. But I am not going to let it consume me. Traveling to the reunion will be a big challenge. But it is so important for me to be there. I really want to be a part of my family, and for small periods of time, I can be."

Mobility

Mobility refers to being able to go where you want to go by walking with or without assistive devices (canes, walkers) or by wheelchair. A variety of conditions can create a need to approach mobility in a different way. Parkinson's disease, arthritis in the knee or hip, back pain, and balance problems such as those occurring after a stroke can all result in changes in mobility. Clearly, if you are depressed and face a problem with how you get around, you are more vulnerable to withdrawing from the world.

One Person's Solution

Wally was the kind of guy whom you wanted to have around when things broke down. He was a real handyman and could fix just about anything, from appliances to plumbing. He was very popular in his retirement apartment building and was always willing to lend a hand in minor repairs for his neighbors. But after developing Parkinson's disease a few years ago, Wally lost his desire to do anything, much less fix broken-down parts. "I felt so broken down myself. My hands shake. My walk was so unsteady and it took me so long to get anywhere. My doctor wanted me to use a walker. I just hated that thing. I felt mortified with it. I was afraid that using it would make me weaker. So I just stopped going anywhere." When his doctor talked to him about depression, Wally agreed and quickly realized that he was not only lonely, but his self-esteem was suffering. He needed to talk with others and find some feeling of usefulness again. He took another look at the dreaded walker. "I decided, if you can't fight 'em, join 'em. Now I carry my toolbox on my walker around the building. I do a few minor repairs, and if my hands are too shaky, I tell them how to do it while I supervise. Since I've been walking more, I actually feel steadier. I'm still slow, but I'm not so worried about that. I'm just so relieved to be out and about."

Hearing and Vision Problems

Any change in these two senses signals "old age" to many. While people who are younger who experience hearing or visual impairment usually adapt to their situation, it can be another matter for older adults who have had a lifetime without these difficulties. For anyone who is hearing impaired, feelings of social isolation and embarrassment about not "being part of things" can be enormous. Visual impairments can be heartbreaking and frightening.

One Person's Solution

Marjorie had taught music to high school students for many decades before she realized that she was losing her hearing. After her husband died when she was sixty-five, Marjorie felt incredibly isolated. She would attend family gatherings and could not hear what other people were saying. She hated her hearing aids and often avoided using them. She stayed home more and more and was often tearful throughout the day, dwelling on the past that she could not go back to. A friend of Marjorie's invited her to come to a depression support group in their area. Marjorie thought that it would be a waste of time because she could not hear. But the group members encouraged Marjorie to wear her hearing aids and even showed her a portable hearing device that made it easier for her to hear some music. Marjorie felt the caring in the group. "The group let me know that it was okay for me to ask them to repeat what they had just said. That meant a lot to me." With the group's encouragement, Marjorie even started attending some band recitals at her old school. "I can't hear as well as I used to, of course. But it means a lot to me to just be surrounded by the music."

Goals to Get You Back in the Swing of Things

Goal 40: Write Back!

Try writing a letter to your condition or to the equipment that you most detest. Start with "Dear (arthritis, pain in my shoulder, wheelchair, C-PAP machine)" and really let it know what you think. Then, approach it with the idea that you will work this out together so that you can get on with your life. Share your letter with your coach and get some feedback.

Dear _____,

_____

_____

_____

_____

_____

Sincerely, _____

Goal 41: Use It or Lose It!

So many people that we meet who are struggling with the challenge of physical health problems and depression have also been to a physical therapist. But when we ask if they are still doing their physical therapy exercises, the answer is very often "no." Physical therapists give you many wonderful exercises that can help you maintain your strength and endurance, but they will not work unless you do them regularly. Your goal is to hunt up those exercises or ask your current physical therapist to give you exercises for the long run. Practice your exercises three days a week for at least five to ten minutes. Keep track of what day and how long you practice on the chart below. After you've kept track of your exercises for a while, doing them should be second nature.

Physical Therapy Practice

	Monday	Tuesday	Wednes-day	Thursday	Friday	Saturday	Sunday
Week 1							
Week 2							
Week 3							
Week 4							

Goal 42: Be Proud of Who You Are

Have you let your condition define who you are? Do you think of yourself as just an extension of an illness? You need to shake up your thinking and remind yourself of all the positive things about who you are. Write some positive affirmations about yourself that include the things that you *can* do. You can also include how well you are managing your physical health. Then say your affirmations aloud, just like you did in chapter 4, and share them with your coach.

Examples: "I go to the store with my son and do my own shopping."

"I remember to take my cane with me wherever I go so that I can stay balanced."

"I manage to take my asthma medications consistently every day."

"I am taking care of my health the best that I can."

Write your own affirmations here:

_____

_____

_____

Goal 43: Become a Fan

Gather stories from magazines, newspapers, and other sources about inspiring people who are dealing with challenging physical conditions. It does not matter if they are young or old, as long as they remind you that many things can be done if you put your mind to it. Put your clippings in a notebook or tape them to the wall where you can look at them and get some daily encouragement and hope. Ask your coach or a family member to keep an eye out for such stories for you. If you are visually impaired, there are many biographies of inspiring people on tape. Check your local library for the blind; tapes can often be sent to you by mail.

Goal 44:   Do a Humor Check

The seriousness of your illness or condition can make you feel like everything in your life is quite somber. Poking fun at your illness or yourself now and then might help to lighten things up a bit. This does not mean you should ridicule yourself; just let some light in on the subject. Practice with your coach. Some suggestions are:

- Some people we know give their pain a name and talk back to it: "There's old Ernie again, giving me trouble!"

- Imagine telling an old friend all the crazy things that you have to do to get out the door. Allow yourself to see things for a moment as silly or ridiculous and let yourself laugh a little. (You can do this with your coach, too.)

- Show other people that you don't take it too seriously. Some people refer to their wheelchair as their "private jet." People with a hearing impairment smile when they ask someone to repeat something and say something like, "I don't want a miss a word that you say!"

- Many people collect written humor and humorous poems about their ailments. Try writing some yourself and share it with your friends.

Goal 45: Jazz Up Your Package

A great coping skill to help you feel more "at home" with your condition and any special equipment that you must use is to put your own special touches on assistive devices. Examples are:

- Dress up your walker or wheelchair with a decorated basket to carry things in. Your special decorative touches are great conversation starters with other people and convey your focus on being positive.

- For balance and good mobility, you may need special shoes or orthotics, or you may need to wear sturdy walking shoes instead of heels. There are many more options than there used to be, so find something that is expressive of you and your style.

- Find a special tote or bag in a fun color or style to carry pads or inhalers, or other larger equipment. Having an accessory that you enjoy can also help you remember to bring things along with you.

Write down some of your own ideas here:

_____

_____

Goal 46: Get in Touch with Your Inner Strength

Your spiritual beliefs can provide great comfort and a different perspective on how to deal with your illness. Here are some ideas to consider:

- Some people, especially when depressed, worry that they are being punished with a disease or problem by a higher power. Talk with your clergyperson to clear the air.

- Attend a service to get in touch with your spirituality.

- Go to a place that provides you with a sense of spirituality, such as a park, the mountains, or the beach. Allow yourself some time to meditate about the goodness in life.

Write down any of these ideas that you can do in the next week:

_____

_____

_____

Every bit of effort that you put into your overall health will help you to gain a sense of control. You will have to take some risks and try new things, but it will pay off in increased confidence and a greater variety of experience.

Chapter 10

Keeping Yourself Healthy and on Track

You have spent time and effort to recover from depression and are seeing blue sky ahead. Now you may be wondering how you stay that way. Making a commitment to your mental health is a lot like taking care of yourself physically. Reaching the goal of recovery is just the beginning of creating a healthy and positive lifestyle. Rest assured that there are many ways that you can maintain control and reduce the likelihood of a relapse of depression.

Phyllis' Story

When Phyllis first experienced depression, she was in her twenties. "We were living in New York at the time. I had lost my mother to cancer and had two young children. I felt overwhelmed and I cried all the time. After a year the crying still wouldn't stop and I couldn't concentrate on anything. My husband insisted that I see a doctor. The doctor told me that I was depressed." Phyllis went to a supportive therapist and slowly recovered.

It was many years later, when Phyllis was in her late fifties, that she became depressed again. Phyllis and her husband had retired early to Florida, but Phyllis found herself longing for her life in the city. "I had all these high hopes for our retirement and I felt very let down. I found things wrong with our new place. I kept comparing the grocery store to the one that I had left back home. I felt so unmotivated. I knew that I needed to get out and make my life there, but it seemed that I had no energy. I felt hopeless and helpless." Phyllis' new doctor recognized the symptoms of depression and suggested that she try an antidepressant and go to a support group. Phyllis reluctantly agreed.

At the support group, Phyllis learned a lot about depression. The group discussed the symptoms and how to recognize them; the participants talked about ways that they could cope with feeling depressed and anxious. The people in the group helped point out the stress that Phyllis was under and how she could cope with it better. "It really helped me understand what was happening to me. The move from New York and all the changes were causing me much more stress than I had realized. It also put things in perspective about the depression that I had had when I was younger." Phyllis also found out about ways that she could keep herself healthy after the depression and that she could take an active stance to keep herself well. She attended the group for a couple of months and then when she felt ready, she stopped going.

About a year after Phyllis recovered from depression, she started to have a setback. "At first, I thought that I was just having some stress because of some problems with my back. One day, I decided to pull out some of my notes from the group. I reviewed the list of symptoms of depression. I thought about how my mood had been over the last few weeks and started to write down some of my thoughts. I called the therapist who ran the group and told her about my concerns. She suggested that I come in for a 'tune-up.'"

Phyllis realizes that it was a good decision. "I think that because I stayed on top of it, the depression did not get as bad as the time before. It took less time to feel better. I plan to check in on myself every now and then and make sure that the 'blues' don't turn into a serious depression again."

The Key to Success: Practicing Relapse Prevention

While some people can have one episode of depression and never have another, the truth is that it is an illness that can return. Some estimates suggest that as many as 50 to 80 percent of people who have one depressive episode can expect to have a recurrence. Sadly, having your first episode with depression later in life makes you more vulnerable to a recurrence (Salzman 1998).

With this in mind, it is vitally important to find ways to minimize the risk of having a recurrence or relapse of this condition. With many of the same principles that you have learned in this book, you can maximize the odds that you will stay well. The concept of relapse prevention should guide you as you continue to recover from depression and as you move beyond the illness. Relapse prevention means:

- You take an active role in maintaining and improving your physical and mental health.

- You regularly monitor yourself for signs of returning symptoms.

- You are actively (not passively) engaged with social supports in your life.

- You have a plan for how you will handle the return of symptoms that includes seeking help *before* symptoms get to a critical point.

- You understand that you have some, but not entire, control over the possibility of a relapse of depression. Symptoms can return in spite of your best effort. You will not condemn yourself if depression returns, but take responsibility to do whatever you can to recover.

Active Steps to Improve Your Chances

As you have been doing the goals in this book to recover from depression, you have probably experienced some changes and progress along the way. Goals are part of the planning process and help ensure that you are paying attention to your day-to-day life and needs. The system of having goals to keep you going in a healthy and positive direction is a good one to continue for relapse prevention.

Here are some basic steps for relapse prevention. These steps will be familiar, as they incorporate the principles that you have already learned by reading the previous chapters:

- **Build your support system.** Nurture relationships and take opportunities to get to know new people in an ongoing way. Your support system should include not only friends and family, and your coach, but also professionals, such as your doctor and therapist. We will discuss the benefits of having a therapist later in the chapter. Have regular contact with your most significant supports, even if it's just a phone call.

- **Know whom you would contact in the event of an emergency,** such as a sudden onset of symptoms or thoughts of suicide. Keep the phone number in an accessible place.

- **Plan your weekly schedule.** Many people fall out of their regular routine when they are depressed. As you recover, you are adding new activities and interests. It is very dangerous to take your schedule for granted and assume that you will do things in a healthy way. It is easy to get sidetracked without a schedule. You might notice that when you write down what you are planning to do, it increases the likelihood that you will follow through and do it. Writing down your schedule in a consistent fashion is an essential relapse prevention tool. There will be a goal to practice this later in the chapter.

• **Check in with yourself.** You should now be the expert on your symptoms, and it is your responsibility to monitor them. When you have recovered from depression, choose a day on the calendar and mark it in. On that day, take a few minutes to rate your mood, anxiety, energy, hopefulness, or other symptoms on a simple scale of good, fair, or bad. Write down your results on the calendar or in a journal. If you notice that you are getting more "fairs" or "bads" than "goods," you know that you need to take active steps. We encourage people who have only recently recovered to do this at least every two weeks. After you have maintained a stable mood for more than a month, you can do this at least once a month. See the goal at the end of the chapter to practice this.

• **Ask others to check in with you.** A trusted family member, your coach, or a friend who knows that you have recovered from depression would be a good candidate for check-ins. Ask this person to let you know if they notice any changes in your mood or behavior. Although you are taking responsibility for your mental health, it does help to have an objective outside view to add to your information.

• **Beware of denial.** If you notice changes, act quickly rather than putting it off. It is usually easier to get back into shape when you have a little depression rather than a very intense, serious depression. Watch out for thoughts such as "I can take care of it myself" or "I'll just keep this to myself." Of course, you should do the self-help steps to feel better, but you need to be honest with yourself when you need more than that. You are an integral part of the recovery process, but your supports are there to help you.

Avoid This Temptation!

After all the hard work you have put into your recovery, you may be tempted to "take a break" from all this mental health stuff. After all, you are probably feeling better and deserve to relax. Relapse prevention does not mean that you must police yourself twenty-four hours a day. But you do need to be aware of how easily you can slip back into behaviors that can re-trigger the same unhappy thoughts and downward mood spiral. Observing yourself, your behavior, and your thoughts takes some discipline but can be well worth it.

Betty's Story

Betty had developed depression following a move from her beloved home that she had helped design to a small retirement apartment in another part of town. She had so many good memories at her old home where she had raised her children and lived the majority of her life. But she had felt overwhelmed by the maintenance and finally gave into her son's encouragement to sell and move into something smaller. She fell into what felt like a dark pit of hopelessness. She couldn't eat. She wanted to sleep all day. She hardly ever bothered to change clothes and slept in whatever she was wearing. When her doctor noticed her decline, he advised her to go to a day treatment program to get help.

The worst part about going to the program for Betty was getting up in time to catch the van. "I have always been a night person and it feels almost like a physical pain to wake up in the morning. I dread it." But somehow she made it each day. Betty had never been in therapy before, but felt relieved to have the support of the staff and the group. She was able to say some of her darkest thoughts out loud and no one rejected her. Slowly, she started to recognize the negative thoughts that she was having and turn them around. Over a couple of months, Betty started to feel better—more motivated and more energetic. Her appetite improved and she was sleeping more regular hours. The staff encouraged Betty to consider getting more active in the community, and Betty remembered a volunteer job at the local food bank that she had been interested in before she had moved. As she prepared to leave the program, Betty assured the group that she would be signing up for the volunteer position.

After Betty completed the program, she felt great. She had really accomplished something important. The first week that she did not go back to the program, she decided to take a breather and sleep in every day. "I wanted a little vacation after I got up early every morning for the program." She promised herself that she would make that call about the volunteer position next week. But when next week came, she found that it was easier to put it off again. It's not like a real job, she thought. There's no commitment. And she was really enjoying just staying in her little apartment more.

In a few months, though, trouble had reappeared. Betty wasn't enjoying staying in her apartment; in fact, it was starting to feel like a prison. But she was too filled with self-doubt to get up the courage to go out. She stopped putting on fresh clothes every day, because, after all, who would see her? She felt ashamed that she had done so well in therapy and now was feeling depressed again.

But when her doctor saw her at her next appointment, he urged her to call the program. A staff person came out to assess Betty at her home and together they confirmed that Betty was having a relapse of depression. Betty arranged to go to a therapist once or twice a week until her symptoms abated. One of her first goals in therapy was to call the food bank and make an appointment to go there to sign up for a volunteer job. "My therapist applauded when I came back with a schedule. It's only a few hours a month, but it's helping me concentrate better and get out of my apartment. It's been a hard lesson, but I realize now that I can't take my health for granted."

When You Need a Helping Hand

Throughout the book, we have noted that therapists can help with depression. There are many good reasons to go to a specialist. There may come a time when you simply need more help in your recovery process, or when you suspect that you are having a relapse. A therapist can be very useful if you have had long-standing stress and conflict in relationships or chronic problems with self-esteem.

Going to a therapist, however, is not a choice that all older adults feel comfortable about making. For some, the thought of going to a therapist brings fear or shame. Perhaps you do not fully understand what exactly happens during therapy and are concerned that it will make you feel worse. You may have an outdated image of therapy that includes, among other things, countless hours of talking about your childhood while reclining on a couch. Therapy these days is quite a bit different from that, and making the choice to go to a therapist can be an invaluable one for many.

Therapy is a helping profession that can move you more quickly toward feeling better. A mental health therapist is a person who is licensed in their state to provide treatment for mental health problems. Training to become a therapist varies depending on the type of licensure the person is seeking and the state in which they live. Therapists work one-on-one or lead groups of individuals who have similar problems and concerns. This helping profession has been around for many years. One way to view therapy is to compare it to any other profession that specializes in helping you to solve a problem. If you have a plumbing problem, you call a plumber. If you have a physical problem, you go see a doctor. If you have psychological problems, you seek the help of a therapist.

It can help to remind yourself of the choices that are yours while you are in therapy:

- You choose what you will discuss in therapy. Your therapist will guide you and will recommend that you explore certain life areas or issues, but ultimately it is your choice.

- You decide which therapist you go to. This is a personal decision and we will give some pointers on how to choose a therapist later in this chapter.

- You can choose to keep therapy brief, with a shorter number of visits. The days of never-ending therapy are long gone, and many studies show that effective therapy can be done in brief periods of time. The length of the therapy is something that you and the therapist should discuss together so that you can get the maximum benefit in a reasonable length of time.

Who Is a Therapist?

Knowing more about each of the professionals who practice therapy will help you to decide whom to go see. Choosing which type of professional you want as your therapist is largely a matter of your specific needs and personal preference. How you relate to a therapist as a person may be more important than what their title is.

Psychiatrists are medical doctors who have specialized in the treatment of mental health problems. Psychiatrists are licensed to provide mental health treatment. As medical doctors they are able to prescribe medications. In contrast to the past, most psychiatrists these days focus primarily on medication management and not on psychotherapy.

Psychologists have earned their doctorate degrees by completing, on average, five years of schooling and practice after college. Psychologists must be licensed in order to practice and have advanced training in psychotherapy and personality and intellectual testing. Psychologists are not able to prescribe medications.

Social Workers are master's level professionals who have two years of training beyond college. They must be licensed to practice therapy independently. They cannot prescribe medications.

Licensed Professional Counselors, Marriage and Family Therapists, School Psychologists, Psychiatric Nurses, and Advanced Practice Nurses all have some training beyond college and must be licensed to practice therapy. In most states, Advanced Practice Nurses can prescribe medications.

There is also a second level of professionals who can help you in times of crisis or need. These include priests, ministers, doctors, lawyers, teachers, nurses, probation officers, consultants, professional life coaches, and others. These professionals may not be trained or licensed to provide therapy, but they can be of enormous help in times of need.

How Therapy Can Help You

Therapy can be viewed as an opportunity to learn how to help yourself. Dr. Steven Hymen, director of the National Institute of Mental Health, puts it this way: "I see psychotherapy as a specialized kind of learning. It's a kind of learning that engages not only our thoughts, but also our emotions, and helps us have either a greater ability in some cases to control our emotions; in other cases a greater ability to live through and handle emotional experiences" (Hymen 1998).

One way to look at therapy is this: If you have ever taken lessons to learn something, you have had the experience of knowing how valuable it can be to have someone show you how to do something. Even people at the peak of their personal and professional lives have a coach to help them achieve more. For example, if you take golf lessons to learn how to play better golf, you will save yourself countless hours of repeating the same mistake over and over again. Tiger Woods still has a teacher to help him with his golf game.

Some of the other benefits of going to a therapist:

- **A therapist has your best interests at heart and can offer you objective support and encouragement.** Talking to family members and friends is valuable, but they are involved in your life. Their concern and caring about you cannot be separated from their personal involvement in your life. A therapist is objective.

- **The therapeutic environment is safe.** When you confide in people close to you, it can affect your relationship in any number of ways. You have probably had the experience of confiding in someone and asking that person to keep the information confidential, only to find out it was not. You edit what you say to friends and family for fear of judgment or criticism. With a therapist, you don't have these concerns and worries.

- **A therapist can challenge you.** A caring, supportive therapist will challenge you to do more than you think you are capable of doing. It's easy to succumb to fatigue and lack of motivation. A good therapist will gently nudge you to take more responsibility for your own recovery and growth.

- **A therapist provides the road map.** If you are in a deep, dark hole and can't see the way out, step-by-step help on how to get out is invaluable. If you feel you are at a crossroads and don't know which road will lead you in the direction you want to go, a therapist can point you in the right direction. You may find yourself lost in the details of your life, whereas your therapist can see the big picture.

Exercise: What Do You Think About Going to a Therapist?

Many older adults have fears or concerns about going to a therapist. These concerns range from questions about privacy or being judged, to fear of not knowing what they will talk about. What are your concerns?

Jim's Story

Jim, a robust and healthy-looking man in his late seventies, has a keen sense of humor and a bravado to go along with it. He was a successful farmer in Kansas managing over 1000 acres and supervising fifteen employees. When Jim reached sixty-five, he decided to sell the farm in order to "give this tired body a break." The sale of his farm left Jim with a very generous retirement and no financial worries. He had divorced his wife more than ten years earlier, and his four children were scattered across the country since "they have no interest in this kind of back-breaking work."

Shortly after retirement Jim started to notice his energy was waning and his usual enthusiasm was dissipating. He began to have thoughts about his wife and how much he missed his children. The abrupt halt to his hectic life was like a gaping hole day after day. Regrets about having sold the farm began to creep into his thinking and before he knew it, he was feeling profound sadness and hopelessness.

Jim finally got up the courage to talk with his doctor about these sudden changes in his life. His doctor suggested that he was having a depressive episode and recommended a therapist in town. Jim's reaction was, "What the hell do I need a shrink for? I've handled things for this long, and I can handle them from here on out."

After two more visits to his doctor with no improvement in his condition, Jim was finally convinced to give the therapist a try. His doctor said, "You can pretty well predict how you will feel if you don't get some help, so why not give it a shot?"

Jim made the appointment and had to admit to himself that for one of the first times in his life he felt fear. He thought, "What will I talk about? How could I have been so successful and feel so helpless now? What will I tell my friends?"

After several visits with his therapist, Jim started to understand and appreciate this special partnership. As he talked about his divorce from his wife, his regrets about retirement, and his estrangement from his children, Jim experienced a tremendous relief. With the help of his therapist, he began to understand how dependent he had become on his work and how over the years it had come to define his personality and identity. His relationships with his wife and children came more clearly into focus, and as difficult as it was to admit, Jim realized that in many respects, he needed to start his life over.

The work that Jim was doing on himself was so different from anything else he had experienced. He commented to his therapist, "and I thought farm work was hard!" But now he knew he was moving forward, with an ally in his corner. His recovery had started and he knew that he had his therapist to count on if he ever started to feel bad again.

Finding the Right Therapist for You

Finding a therapist that you can trust, feel comfortable with, and make progress with is not always easy. There are several places to begin your search. Here are a few:

- Ask friends, colleagues, church members, or relatives if they know of someone good. But be aware that a therapist that someone else recommends may not necessarily be the right one for you.

- Locate your local psychological association or social work organization and get a list of therapists who work with older adults and who accept your insurance.

- Contact your local Area Agency on Aging or Aging Services program to inquire about therapists.

- Ask your doctor to recommend a therapist.

- If you are from a particular ethnic or cultural group, look to organizations that represent those groups to find a therapist. If you are gay or lesbian you may prefer a therapist who works with those groups. Look at publications catering to these groups and you will probably find therapists advertised there.

- Look in the phone book.

- If at all possible, try to find a therapist who has experience with and works consistently with older adults. There are issues, concerns, and circumstances that are unique to older adults. Someone who is not sensitive to these characteristics will not be as effective in helping you. Ask a prospective therapist about their experience in the area of aging.

- Interview more than one therapist, if you can, before you make a final decision. This can be done in a simple phone conversation.

- Trust your instincts. If someone doesn't feel right for you, despite how well recommended they come, then move on.

- Talk with your therapist about what your therapy schedule will be. Some people go every week and others go once a month or anything else in between.

- A therapist is not your friend in a traditional sense. It is more appropriate to think of them as your partner in the recovery process. Your therapist might challenge or gently confront you about your thoughts, feelings, or behavior. You may not like it, but you should acknowledge that this could be very helpful to your recovery process.

- Don't expect miracles. It takes time for therapy to help you feel better. Your unique journey will be different from anyone else's, so don't compare yourself to someone else. Therapy is a partnership, and a therapist needs your active involvement to help you.

- If after a certain amount of time, you don't feel that you are making progress, talk to your therapist about it. You have a right to ask your therapist how long they anticipate you will be in therapy.

"Can I Afford to Go to a Therapist?"

A therapist's fee will vary from state to state, and will also depend on what type of license they have. If you have private insurance, it behooves you to contact your insurance group to find out the names of therapists who are covered under your plan. That way, insurance will pick up part of the cost of therapy, but you will still be responsible for a co-pay.

If you are on Medicare, the picture is a bit more challenging. Medicare does not reimburse therapists at as high a rate as many private insurance companies; therefore many therapists choose not to become Medicare providers. You must ask a therapist if they accept Medicare insurance unless you are prepared to pay the entire cost of therapy yourself or negotiate a fee that you both agree upon.

Goals for Relapse Prevention

This final batch of goals will help guide you through future challenges. Consider referring to this section on a regular basis after you reach your recovery goals.

Goal 47: Your Needs and the Goals to Help You Succeed

As you plan for your recovery and maintaining good mental health, you must practice being aware of your needs in each area of your life. Beside each area listed below, make one statement for each category that characterizes your need in that area. Then beside it, make a positive goal statement that moves you forward from that need. For example, a need statement might be: "I need to take better care of myself physically." A goal statement might be: "I am starting (or will start) an exercise program to improve my health." Another need statement: "I need to get out and meet more people." A goal statement might be: " I have increased (or will increase) my social activity by visiting the senior center once a week." If you have already made a start on a goal, go ahead and write it beside the need. Think of this as a summary of all the work you have done thus far in the book. It will also indicate possible starting places for you to explore in therapy.

Self-Esteem

Need: _____

Goal: _____

Physical Health

Need: _____

Goal: _____

Nutrition

Need: _____

Goal: _____

Social Connections

Need: _____

Goal: _____

Grief and Loss

Need: _____

Goal: _____

Community Resources

Need: _____

Goal: _____

Relapse Prevention

Need: _____

Goal: _____

Goal 48: Planning Your Schedule

Planning your schedule takes time and thought. A major priority in this endeavor is to achieve balance. Some people recovering from depression have the urge to make up for lost time, so they overbook their schedules. For others, the depression may still be present to some degree and that discourages them from planning enough activities during the week. Consider the list below of areas of your life that should be included in your weekly schedule. Then practice adding specific activities that you do in those life areas to your schedule. You may want to try a couple of different schedules before you settle on one. It is all right if there is some repetition, and you should not try to fill each block of space completely. Avoid having more than two whole days in a week with nothing planned. This should be an indicator to you that you need to do some more planning.

Life Activity Areas and Examples:

Daily Tasks
housecleaning
laundry
grocery shopping

Relaxation
deep breathing
face massage
singing

Recreation
travel
sports
cards

Social Activities
family gatherings
going to the senior center
clubs

Intellectual Stimulation
reading
classes
crossword puzzles

Exercise
walking
swimming
tennis

Spirituality
place of worship
meditation
prayer

Monday	Tuesday	Wednesday	Thursday	Friday	Saturday	Sunday
Morning:	Morning:	Morning:	Morning:	Morning:	Morning:	Morning:
Afternoon:	Afternoon:	Afternoon:	Afternoon:	Afternoon:	Afternoon:	Afternoon:
Evening:	Evening:	Evening:	Evening:	Evening:	Evening:	Evening:

Goal 49: Checking In to Stay On Track

You don't have to obsess about your symptoms returning in order to stay clued in to your mental health. By simply rating your possible symptoms on a regular basis, you can improve your awareness of how you are feeling and stay on top of your mental health. Refer to the list of symptoms of depression in chapter 1. Rate the symptoms that were most significant for you. (Note that it is important, however, to review the whole list. You may have different symptoms of depression from one episode to the next.) Remember, if you have recently recovered from your symptoms of depression, do this at least once a week. Later, you can move to once a month. Mark a consistent day on the calendar, such as the first or last day of the week or month, to do this routinely. Examples:

Mood

Bad   Fair   Good

Appetite

Bad   Fair   Good

Sleep

Bad   Fair   Good

Energy

Bad   Fair   Good

Goal 50: Practice Damage Control

Imagine that you have been in recovery for many months and you start to notice the return of symptoms. What is your damage-control plan? Write down what your steps will be, from whom you will call for assistance to how you can increase your practice of ideas that you have learned from this book:

\

\

\

====

Goal 51: On the Hunt for a Good Therapist

====

If you are choosing to go to a therapist, make four phone calls this week to ask about good therapists. Consider all of the suggestions we have made such as clergy, your doctor, therapy associations, and aging services. Keep track of the therapists' names and phone numbers and any other relevant information.

\

\

\

====

Goal 52: Finding the Right Therapist for You

====

Write down all of the questions that you would like to ask a potential therapist. These questions may include:

- "What type of license do you have?"

- "What is your therapeutic approach?"

- "How is payment handled?"

- "Are you experienced in working with older adults?"

What other questions do you have for the therapist? Write them down here:

_____

_____

_____

_____

Role-play these questions with your coach. Then make your calls. After making each call, write down your impressions of the therapist.

Therapist name: _____

Impression: _____

Therapist name: _____

Impression: _____

With a clear decision and some planning, you can take charge of your emotional well-being. The concepts of relapse prevention can guide your choices for a healthy and happy lifestyle. Be sure to congratulate yourself on putting in the effort that you have given to your recovery.

Recommended Readings and Resources

Chapter 1

Suggested Readings

American Psychiatric Association. 2000. *Diagnostic and Statistical Manual of Mental Disorders. Fourth Edition, Text Revision.* Washington, D.C.: American Psychiatric Association.

Department of Health and Human Services. 1999. *Mental Health: A Report of the Surgeon General.* www.surgeongeneral.gov/library/mentalhealth

Friedan, B. 1993. *The Fountain of Age.* New York: Simon and Schuster.

Hales, D., and R. Hales. 1995. *Caring for the Mind: The Comprehensive Guide to Mental Health.* New York: Bantam Books.

National Institute of Mental Health. *If You're Over 65 and Feeling Depressed: Treatment Brings New Hope.* www.nimh.nih.gov/publicat/over65.

Zalman, S. 1997. *From Age-ing to Sage-ing: A Profound New Vision of Growing Older.* New York: Warner Books.

Resources

Geriatric Psychiatry Alliance
1201 Connecticut Avenue, #300
Washington, DC 20036
(888) INFO-GPA

National Alliance for the Mentally Ill
Colonial Place Three
2107 Wilson Blvd., Suite 300
Arlington, VA 22201-3042
(703) 524-7600; (800) 950-NAMI
Web site: http://www.nami.org

National Depressive and Manic Depressive Association
730 N. Franklin, Suite 501
Chicago, IL 60601
(312) 642-0049; (800) 826-3632
Web site: http://www.ndmda.org

National Foundation for Depressive Illness, Inc.
P.O. Box 2257
New York, NY 10016
(212) 268-4260; (800) 239-1265
Web site: http://www.depression.org

National Institute of Mental Health
Office of Communications and Public Liaison, NIMH
Information Resources and Inquiries Branch
6001 Executive Blvd., Room 8184, MSC 9663
Bethesda, MD 20892-9663
(301) 443-4513
Fax: (301) 443-4279
Mental Health Fax 4U: (301) 443-5158
TTY: (301) 443-8431
E-mail: nimhinfo@nih.gov
NIMH Web site: http://www.nimh.nih.gov

National Mental Health Association
1021 Prince Street
Alexandria, VA 22314-2971
(703) 684-7722; (800) 696-6642
Fax: (703) 684-5968
TTY: (800) 433-5959
Web site: http://www.nmha.org

Reclamation, Inc.
2502 Waterford
San Antonio, TX 78217
(512) 824-8618

Recovery, Inc.
802 North Dearborn ST.
Chicago, IL 60610
(312) 337-5661

Chapter 3

Suggested Readings

Rowe, J., and R. L. Kahn. 1998. *Successful Aging*. New York: Pantheon Books.

Resources

Administration on Aging
330 Independence Avenue SW
Washington DC 20201
(800) 677-1116

American Association of Homes and Services for the Aging
901 E St. NW
Washington, DC 20004-2037
(202) 783-2242
Web-site: www.aahsa.org

American College of Health Care Administrators
Offers continuing education, professional certification programs for assisted living, nursing homes, and more.
325 S. Patrick St.
Alexandria, VA 22314
(888) 88A-CHCA
Web site: www.info@achca.org

American Society on Aging
833 Market Street, Suite 511
San Francisco, CA 94103-1824

Area Agencies on Aging
To locate resources in your area, including senior centers, call: (800) 677-1116. Web site address for *state* agencies on aging: http://www.aoa.dhhs.gov/aoa/pages/state.tml.

Assisted Living Federation of America (AHCA)
9401 Lee Highway, Suite 402
Fairfax, VA 22031
(703) 691-8100

Elderhostel
11 Avenue de Lafayette
Boston, MA 02111-1746
Phone: (877) 426-8056

Gerontological Society of America
1275 K St. NW, Suite 350
Washington, DC 20005-4006
(202) 842-1275

Mail Station
E-mail appliance that provides e-mail service only. A personal computer is not needed. They average about $100 plus monthly access fee. Available at most electronics stores

National Council on Aging
409 Third St. SW, Suite 200
Washington DC 20024
(202) 479-1200
Web site: www.nco.org

Chapter 4

Suggested Readings

Bourne, Edmund J. 2001. *Beyond Anxiety & Phobia*. Oakland, Calif.: New Harbinger Publications.

Branden, Nathaniel. 1987. *How to Raise Your Self-Esteem*. New York: Bantam Books.

Copeland, Mary Ellen. 2001. *The Depression Workbook: A Guide for Living with Depression and Manic Depression*. Second Edition. Oakland, Calif.: New Harbinger Publications.

Chapter 5

Suggested Readings

Albom, Mitch. 1997. *Tuesdays with Morrie*. New York: Doubleday.

Brothers, Joyce. 1991. *Widowed*. New York: Ballantine Books.

Campbell, S., and P. Silverman. 1987. *Widower: What Happens When Men Are Left Alone*. New York: Prentice Hall.

Carrol, David. 1989. *When Your Loved One Has Alzheimer's*. New York: Harper & Row.

Irish, D., K. Lundquist, V. J. Nelsen, eds. 1993. *Ethnic Variations in Dying, Death, and Grief: Diversity in Universality*. Washington, D.C.: Taylor & Francis, Inc.

Klass, Dennis, Phyllis R. Silverman, and Steven L. Nichman. 1996. *Continuing Bonds: New Understanding of Grief*. Washington, D.C.: Taylor and Francis.

Kubler-Ross, Elisabeth. 1997. *The Wheel of Life: A Memoir of Living and Dying*. New York: Scribner.

_____. 1997. *Death: The Final Stage of Growth*. New York: Simon and Schuster.

_____. 1995. *Death Is of Vital Importance*. New York: Station Hill.

_____. 1991. *On Life After Death*. Berkeley, Calif.: Celestial Arts.

_____. 1981. *Living With Death and Dying*. New York: Macmillan.

_____. 1969. *On Death and Dying*. New York: Macmillan.

Kushner, Harold. 1981. *When Bad Things Happen to Good People*. New York: Schocken Brothers.

Leming, Michael R., and George E. Dicksen. 1998. *Understanding Dying, Death, and Bereavement*. Orlando, Fla.: Harcourt Brace and Company.

Levine, Stephen. 1982. *Who Dies?* New York: Doubleday.

Lund, Dale A., editor. 2001. *Men Coping with Grief*. Amityville, N.Y.: Baywood Publishing.

_____. 1989. *Older Bereaved Spouses*. Washington, D.C.: Taylor Francis/Hemisphere.

Segal, Jeanne. 1989. *Living Beyond Fear: Coping with the Emotional Aspects of Life-Threatening Illness*. New York: Ballantine.

Staudacher, Carol. 1994. *A Time to Grieve: Meditations for Healing After the Death of a Loved One*. New York: HarperCollins.

_____. 1987. *Beyond Grief: A Guide for Recovering from the Death of a Loved One*. Oakland, Calif.: New Harbinger Publications.

Weenolsen, Patricia. 1996. *The Art of Dying*. New York: St. Martin's Press.

Chapter 6

Suggested Readings

Hales, Dianne R., and Robert E. Hales. 2000. *The Mind/Mood Pill Book*. New York: Bantam Doubleday Dell Publishers.

Silverman, Harold. 2000. *The Pill Book. Ninth Edition*. New York: Bantam Books.

Tyler, Varro E. 1994. *Herbs of Choice: the Therapeutic Use of Phytomedicinals*. New York: Pharmaceutical Products Press. An imprint of The Haworth Press, Inc.

Resources

National Alliance of the Mentally Ill
Colonial Place Three
2107 Wilson Blvd., Suite 300
Arlington, VA 22201-3042
(703) 524-7600; (800) 950-NAMI
Web site: http://www.nami.org
Web page of patient assistance programs: http://www.nami.org/helpline/freemed.htm
A tremendous resource for finding help in your community for mental health concerns.

The Medicine Program
P.O. Box 520
Doniphan, MO 63935-0520
(533) 996-7300
Web site: www.themedicineprogram.com
For a small fee, this program will gather all of the applications for patient assistance programs for the drugs that you are taking and send them to you.

Pharmaceutical Research and Manufacturers of America
Web site: www.phrma.org
For further information about specific patient assistance programs of the major drug companies.

Medication	Drug Company	Phone Number
Celexa	Forest Laboratories	800/678-1605 ext 207
Depakote	Abbott Laboratories	800/441-4987
Desyrel	Bristol-Myers Squibb Company	800/332-2056
Effexor	Wyeth-Ayerst Laboratories	800/568-9938
Luvox	Solvay Pharmaceuticals, Inc.	800/788-9277

Medication	Drug Company	Phone Number
Paxil	SmithKline Beecham Pharmaceuticals	800/546-0420
Prozac	Eli Lilly and Company	800/545-6962
Remeron	Organon	800/241-8812
Serzone	Bristol-Myers Squibb Company	800/332-2056
Wellbutrin	Glaxo Wellcome Inc.	800/722-9294
Zoloft	Pfizer Inc.	800/646-4455

Chapter 7

Suggested Readings

Bourne, Edmund J. 2001. *The Anxiety and Phobia Workbook. Third Edition*. Oakland, Calif.: New Harbinger Publications.

_____. 2001. *Beyond Anxiety & Phobia*. Oakland, Calif.: New Harbinger Publications.

Davis, Martha, Elizabeth R. Eshelman, and Matthew McKay. 2001. *The Relaxation and Stress Reduction Workbook. Fifth Edition*. Oakland, Calif.: New Harbinger Publications.

Resources

Video and Audio Tapes

Johnson, Mark. 1995. *Tai Chi for Seniors*. The Tai Chi for Health Institute. 59 minutes. This very popular video includes 30 minutes of gentle Tai Chi movements, broken down into 10 simple forms. The remainder of the video has techniques and exercises to improve overall health.

The Tai Chi for Health Institute
30 Elaine Avenue
Mill Valley, CA 94941
(800) 497-4244
Web site: www.chi-kung.com

The Redbook Workout Series. 1994. *Tai Chi*. Troy, Michigan. Video Treasures, Inc.

Very pleasant visual setting and easy-to-follow, encouraging instructions. If you enjoy the face massage we described, you will like additional similar exercises on this tape.

Redfield, Salle Merrill. 1995. *The Joy of Meditating*. Cassette tape. Los Angeles: Time Warner AudioBooks.

Soothing female voice guides you through deep breathing and simple visualization exercises. Approximately 60 minutes but can be listened to in 10–15 minute segments.

Yoga Music and Video
P.O. Box 769689
Roswell, Georgia 30076
(800) 878-4764
Web Site: www.yogamusicvideo.com

This resource offers a variety of yoga videos from beginner to advanced and also soothing music for yoga or stress reduction.

Chapter 8

Suggested Readings

Chopra, Deepak. 1993. *Ageless Body, Timeless Mind*. New York: Harmony Books.

Margen, Sheldon. 1992. *The Wellness Encyclopedia of Food and Nutrition: How to Buy, Store, and Prepare Every Variety of Fresh Food*. New York: Random House.

White, Timothy, and the Editors of the University of California at Berkeley Wellness Center. 1993. *The Wellness Guide to Lifelong Fitness*. New York: Random House.

Resources

Exercise: A Guide from the National Institute on Aging
NIAIC, Dept. M-P Box 8057
Gaithersburg, MD 20898
Web site: www.nih.gov/nia/health/pubs/nasa-exercise/

The Food Guide Pyramid
The United States Department of Agriculture
Web site: www.nal.usda.gov/

AARP (American Association of Retired Persons)
Membership information:
AARP
P.O. Box 199
Long Beach, CA 90801
Web site: www.aarp.org

American Cancer Society
(800) ACS-2345
Web site: www.cancer.org

American College of Sports Medicine
ACSM National Center
P.O. Box 1440
Indianapolis, IN 46206-1440
Web site: www.acsm.org

American Diabetes Association
(800) Diabetes (342-2383)
Web site: www.diabetes.org

American Dietetic Association
Consumer Education Team
216 West Jackson Blvd.
Chicago, IL 60606
(800) 366-1655
Web site: www.eatright.org

American Heart Association
(800) AHA-USA1
(888) 4-STROKE
(888) MY-HEART
Web site: www.americanheart.org

Food and Nutrition Institute
10301 Baltimore Avenue
Beltsville, MD 20705
(301) 504-5755
Web site: www.nal.usda.gov/fnic/

Mayo Clinic
200 First Street SW
Rochester, MN 55905
Web site: www.mayohealth.org

National Cancer Institute
Web site: www.Rex.nci.nih.gov

National Institute of Diabetes and Digestive and Kidney Diseases
NIDDK, NIH
31 Center Drive, MSC 2560
Bethesda, MD 20892-2560

Tufts University Nutrition
Web site: www.navigator.tufts.edu

The Surgeon General's Report on Exercise, Diet and Older Adults
Web site: www.cdc.gov/nccdphp/sgr/summary

Chapter 9

Resources

Occupational Therapy

Talk with your health-care provider to find out if you qualify for the services of an occupational therapist. They have wonderful skills in helping you find ways to do your daily tasks with greater ease. Find out more about occupational therapists in your area by looking under "Occupational Therapy" in your yellow pages, or contact:

The American Occupational Therapists Association, Inc.
Web site: www.aota.org/

Radio Shack 3-Band Equalizer Stereo Amplified Listener
This economical, portable hearing device combined with a headset of your choice can greatly improve your ability to hear others speaking. It has made an amazing difference for people in our groups who are hearing impaired. Even some people who wear hearing aids have found this to be helpful.

Chapter 10

Suggested Readings

Mental Health: A Report of the Surgeon General. 1999. Professional Web site: www.surgeongeneral.gov/library/mentalhealth/

Resources

American Academy of Nurse Practitioners
P.O. Box 12846
Austin, TX 78711
(512) 442-4262

American Psychiatric Association
1400 K Street NW
Washington, DC 20005
(888) 357-7924

American Psychological Association
750 First Street NE
Washington, DC 20002-4242
(202) 336-5500

National Association of Social Workers
750 First Street NE, Suite 700
Washington, DC 20002-4242
(800) 638-8799

References

Albom, Mitch. 1997. *Tuesdays with Morrie*. New York: Doubleday.

All Things Considered. 1998. National Public Radio. "Therapy vs. Drugs Part 1." June 22

American Psychiatric Association. 1994. *Diagnostic and Statistical Manual of Mental Disorders. Fourth Edition*. Washington, D.C.: American Psychiatric Association.

Bottiglieri, T., K. Hyland, E. H. Reynolds, 1994. The Clinical Potential of Ademetionine (S-ademosylmethionine) in Neurological Disorders. *Drugs* 48(2): 137–52.

Bourne, Edmund J. 2000. *The Anxiety and Phobia Workbook, Third Edition*. Oakland, Calif.: New Harbinger Publications.

_____. 2001. *Beyond Anxiety & Phobia*. Oakland, Calif.: New Harbinger Publications.

Branden, Nathaniel. 1987. *How to Raise Your Self-Esteem*. New York: Bantam Books.

Brothers, Joyce. 1991. *Widowed*. New York: Ballantine Books.

Chopra, Deepak. 1993. *Ageless Body, Timeless Mind*. New York: Harmony Books.

Copeland, Mary Ellen. 2001. *The Depression Workbook: A Guide for Living with Depression and Manic Depression. Second Edition*. Oakland, Calif.: New Harbinger Publications.

Davis, Martha, Elizabeth R. Eshelman, Matthew McKay. 2001. *The Relaxation and Stress Reduction Workbook. Fifth Edition*. Oakland, Calif.: New Harbinger Publications.

Department of Health and Human Services. 1999. *Mental Health: A Report of the Surgeon General*. www.surgeongeneral.gov/library/mentalhealth

Hales, Dianne, and Robert E. Hales. 1995. *Caring for the Mind: The Comprehensive Guide to Mental Health*. New York: Bantam Books.

Hymen, Steven. *All Things Considered*. 1998. National Public Radio. "Therapy vs. Drugs Part 1." June 22.

Irish, D., K. Lundquist, V. J. Nelsen, eds. 1993. *Ethnic Variations in Dying, Death, and Grief: Diversity in Universality*. Washington, D.C.: Taylor & Francis, Inc.

Jacobs, D. G. 2000. *What Are the Signs and Symptoms of Depression?* National Depression Screening Day Lecture. www.nmuso.org/dep/

Lund, Dale, A. 1996. Grieving in later life: Some advice that might help. *Excellence*. Fall.

Margen, Sheldon. 1992. *The Wellness Encyclopedia of Food and Nutrition: How to Buy, Store and Prepare Every Variety of Fresh Food*. New York: Random House.

Mosby's GenRx, The Complete Reference for Generic and Brand Drugs. Eighth Edition. 1998. New York: Mosby.

National Depressive and Manic-Depressive Association. www.ndmda.org

National Institutes of Health. *Exercise: A Guide from the National Institute on Aging*. www.nih.gov/nia/health/pubs/nasa-exercise/htm

National Institutes of Health. 2001. *Exercise: A Guide from the National Institute on Aging*. Chapter 6: "What Should I Eat? Supplements: Costly and Not Necessarily Helpful." 4–5.

National Institute of Mental Health. *If You're Over 65 and Feeling Depressed: Treatment Brings New Hope*. www.nimh.nih.gov/publicat/over65

National Mental Health Association. *Dysthymia*. www.nmha.org/infoctr/factsheets/26.cfm

National Osteoporosis Foundation. 2001. Disease Statistics. www.nof.org/osteoporosis/stats/htm

Puzantian, Talia, and Glen L. Stimmel. 2001. *Review of Psychotropic Drugs*. CNS News Special Edition. New York: McMahon Publishing Group.

Rowe, J., and R. L. Kahn. 1998. *Successful Aging*. New York: Pantheon Books.

Salzman, Carl, ed. 1998. *Clinical Geriatric Pharmacology. Third Edition.* Baltimore, Md.: Williams and Wilkens.

Shelton, Richard, Martin Keller, Alan Gelenburg, David Dunner, Robert Hirshfeld, et al. 2001. Effectiveness of St. John's wort in major depression: A randomized controlled trial. *Journal of the American Medical Association* 285(15).

Segal, Jeanne. 1989. *Living Beyond Fear: Coping with the Emotional Aspects of Life-Threatening Illness.* New York: Ballantine.

Stahl, Stephen M. 1997. *Psychopharmacology of Antidepressants.* London: Martin Dunitz, Ltd.

Staudacher, Carol. 1987. *Beyond Grief: A Guide for Recovering from the Death of a Loved One.* Oakland, Calif: New Harbinger Publications.

Tyler, Varro E. 1994. *Herbs of Choice: The Therapeutic Use of Phytomedicinals.* New York: Pharmaceutical Products Press. An imprint of The Haworth Press, Inc.

White, Timothy, and the Editors of the University of California at Berkeley Wellness Center. 1993. *The Wellness Guide to Lifelong Fitness.* New York: Random House.

 **Amanda Lambert, M.S.,** is a specialist in the senior mental health community and the President of the Utah Gerontological Society.

Leslie Eckford is a licensed clinical social worker and a psychiatric  nurse. She specializes in geriatric psychiatry.

Many of their senior clients have had positive results using the advice and methods described in this book.

You can visit the authors at their website: www.mindfulaging.com.

Some Other
New Harbinger Titles

Do-It-Yourself Eye Movement Technique for Emotional Healing, Item DIYE $13.95

Stop the Anger Now, Item SAGN $17.95

The Self-Esteem Workbook, Item SEWB $18.95

The Habit Change Workbook, Item HBCW $19.95

The Memory Workbook, Item MMWB $18.95

The Anxiety & Phobia Workbook, 3rd edition, Item PHO3 $19.95

Beyond Anxiety & Phobia, Item BYAP $19.95

The Self-Nourishment Companion, Item SNC $10.95

The Healing Sorrow Workbook, Item HSW $17.95

The Daily Relaxer, Item DALY $12.95

Stop Controlling Me!, Item SCM $13.95

Lift Your Mood Now, Item LYMN $12.95

An End to Panic, 2nd edition, Item END2 $19.95

Serenity to Go, Item STG $12.95

The Depression Workbook, Item DEP $19.95

The OCD Workbook, Item OCDWK $18.95

The Anger Control Workbook, Item ACWB $17.95

Flying without Fear, Item FLY $14.95

The Shyness & Social Anxiety Workbook, Item SHYW $16.95

The Relaxation & Stress Reduction Workbook, 5th edition, Item RS5 $19.95

Energy Tapping, Item ETAP $15.95

Stop Walking on Eggshells, Item WOE $15.95

Angry All the Time, Item ALL 13.95

Living without Procrastination, Item LWD $12.95

Hypnosis for Change, 3rd edition, Item HYP3 $16.95

Toxic Coworkers, Item TOXC $13.95

Letting Go of Anger, Item LET $13.95

Call **toll free, 1-800-748-6273,** or log on to our online bookstore at **www.newharbinger.com** to order. Have your Visa or Mastercard number ready. Or send a check for the titles you want to New Harbinger Publications, Inc., 5674 Shattuck Ave., Oakland, CA 94609. Include $4.50 for the first book and 75¢ for each additional book, to cover shipping and handling. (California residents please include appropriate sales tax.) Allow two to five weeks for delivery.

Prices subject to change without notice.